nom nom nom ITALY 5 IN INGREDIENTS

Delicious Italian inspired meals with just 5 ingredients

Cooked in 15 minutes or less

nom nom ITALY IN 5 INGREDIENTS

Delicious Italian inspired meals with just 5 ingredients. Cooked in 15 minutes or less.

Copyright © Iota Publishing Limited 2019

Images under licence from Shutterstock

ISBN: 978-1913005-06-1

DISCLAIMER

This book is designed to provide information on Italian inspired cuisine. Some recipes may contain nuts or traces of nuts. Those suffering from any allergies associated with nuts should avoid any recipes containing nuts or nut based oils.

This information is provided and sold with the knowledge that the publisher and author do not offer any legal or other professional advice.
In the case of a need for any such expertise consult with the appropriate professional.
This book does not contain all information available on the subject, and other sources of recipes are available.
Every effort has been made to make this book as accurate as possible. However, there may be typographical and or content errors. Therefore, this book should serve only as a general guide and not as the ultimate source of subject information.
This book contains information that might be dated and is intended only to educate and entertain.

contents

Pizza 75

Conversion Chart

nom nom
to eat something with great enjoyment

Inspired by the simplicity of Italian food, we offer a fantastic selection of truly traditional recipes that are not just quick and easy to prepare and cook, but are composed of 5 familiar ingredients.

This selection of quick and easy yet delicious recipes are designed to complement our busy lifestyles. Whilst there are some fabulous cook books available many require pre-planning, preparation prior to cooking, or include a number of ingredients unlikely to be in your cupboard! For everyday meals, who honestly has the time to caramelise garlic 3 hours before cooking? Or marinade and leave meat to rest for 6 hours prior to placing in the oven? Whilst such methods are, of course, suitable in some scenarios, this brilliant range of recipes are fast and specially designed to offer you fantastic flavours for minimal effort.

The secret to success is the quality of the 5 ingredients you use. Quality is something which should never be compromised on. Using fewer ingredients means each individual component gets its chance to shine and the balance of flavours will be lost if the quality is not there.

In general, the UK is particularly bad at buying too many pre-prepared meals; from frozen pizzas to pastas sauces and salad dressings, all of these products with long shelf lives are contributing to an increasingly unhealthy lifestyle, as well as record numbers of digestive issues, across the country. Processed foods are very difficult for our bodies to digest and once we have suffered the bloat and discomfort, our bodies often still do not know what to do with the artificial elements so store them as excess fat. The key to combatting this is to truly go back to basics and prepare these meals from scratch, or as far as possible. The difficulty is that this can be time consuming and intimidating, even for confident cooks. However cooking does not need to be this way!

That is why we simplify things right down to the basic, core elements in a fuss-free range of recipes that are almost certain to get you excited in the kitchen by using wondrous flavours but refreshingly easy methods.

'Like mother used to make' is a phrase we are hearing more and more - it's often seen splashed across recipe books, in an attempt to encourage even the least natural of cooks to begin preparing more meals from scratch, using fresh, or even better, local, ingredients as much as possible. Whilst this is incredibly positive and absolutely encouraged, the reality of the situation is that many of us quite simply do not have the time. Managing a work and home life balance, busy lifestyles and trying to somehow squeeze everything we need and are meant to do in a day is just chaos in itself. Cooking should be enjoyable, yet many fear it like a burden.
Too many recipes take too much time prepare, or include huge lists of ingredients that, when you do finally have time to think about cooking, requires a trip to the supermarket before you can even get started.

European cuisines can hold a great deal of inspiration when looking for simple, healthy meals made from the simplest of ingredients. Italian cuisine in particular is excellent at offering a delicious variety of traditional dishes that may often look luxuriously extravagant, but are actually composed of a very simple selection of fresh, quality ingredients.

Italian meals are often plant-based and it no doubt comes as little surprise that a crucial component of Italian cooking, and essentially easy cooking, is the tomato. The tomato is perhaps the holy grail of Italian cookery, forming the base of many pasta sauces and pizzas, and a regular marinade for fish and meat. Additionally, tomatoes come with an incredible range of health benefits; they have been linked to helping reduce and prevent some cancers and are wonderfully rich in antioxidants, like many other staple Italian ingredients. They are incredibly versatile, serve a wide range of purposes and can be adapted to produce a huge variety of flavours, but furthermore, they are so brilliantly simple to work with and store. Tinned tomatoes are possibly one of the best, if not the best, item to have in your cupboard, for all of the above reasons.
As wonderful as fresh food is, it is no secret that it does not keep for very long and we may not always have the time to pick up fresh ingredients each day.

The tinned variety can be just as nutritious, is easier to work with, and has a truly excellent shelf life.

Off-the-shelf pasta sauces are packed with preservatives and artificial ingredients which push up calorie content, are often drenched in sugar and rich in unnecessary additives that hinder digestion and hang on to your hips. Going back to basics really does work wonders and makes the biggest difference to your health. When switching to homemade sauces, many people report noticeable digestive improvements; they perhaps previously thought it was in fact pasta that was leaving them bloated, uncomfortable and unable to shift excess weight, yet it quickly becomes apparent that it was actually the sauce. Many staple Italian foods are excellent anti-inflammatories and contain a wealth of nutrients, as well as antioxidants. We provide a fabulous selection of traditional pasta dishes from simple tomato penne to seafood linguine, all of which can be quickly, and easily, whipped up at home and are almost guaranteed to be much simpler than you probably ever expected.

We bring you the best of Italy with just five key ingredients per recipe. Our recipes list the 5 ingredients you will need to buy in specially for the recipe, but they assume you have a range of store cupboard items to hand to accompany them.
Your essential store cupboard ingredients (which many of our recipes use, but won't be listed as ingredients) are:

tinned tomatoes
olive oil,
salt and pepper,
garlic cloves,
balsamic vinegar
tomato puree

They really do underpin the very essence of cooking, particular with Italian, and enable you to create an incredible range of flavours from such simple essentials. So, if they are not already hidden in your cupboard, put them on your shopping list now!

The 5 key ingredients in each of our recipes work fabulously together and really simplify a recipe to its core. They are perfect for anybody to try, regardless of your cooking experience or ability. Whether cooking for yourself, family or friends, these gorgeously nutritious meals are bursting with flavour and can easily be adapted to suit your preferences; like things hot? Throw in a little more chilli! Prefer a creamy sauce? Add some crème fraiche and a splash of white wine. These recipes are so easy to play around with that even the most novice of cooks will begin to feel confident in experimenting in the kitchen and deviating from the traditional in no time at all. Playing with flavour is ultimately the Italian way and these recipes are an excellent range of ideas to get you started. With the limited number of ingredients, this is an easy way to involve children in cooking too, making it a fun way to prepare the family meals in a wholesome, educational and healthy way.

Whilst many recipes form an entire meal, some are just inspiring ways to marinate fish or meat, and are best served with a side of seasonal vegetables. The beauty of Italian cuisine is that everything is so versatile, making it wonderfully easy to simply add linguine to a fish dish to provide a more balanced meal, or throw some roasted root vegetables on top of a pizza to help boost your five a day. This stunning range of Italian ideas can act as your base for every day meals, and, when entertaining friends, the selection of antipasti can be easily adapted into larger platters to wow the crowd impressing them with delicious sides, snacks and nibbles to enjoy before dinner or with a cold, crisp glass of wine.

There really are no excuses to not dive straight in today to begin exploring the culinary delights of Italy and indulging in its delicious simplicity.

nom
nom
ITALY
anti pasti

Green Chilli Salsa

- 2 large tomatoes, finely diced
- ½ red onion, peeled and finely diced
- 1 green chilli, de-seeded and finely diced
- ½ tsp freshly squeezed lime juice
- 1 tsp fresh coriander, finely chopped

- Place the chopped tomato, onion and chilli in a bowl and toss together.

- Add in either half a clove of minced garlic, or one very small clove of minced garlic, and mix well. Drizzle in a little extra virgin olive oil, along with the freshly squeezed lime juice then stir the salsa together.

- Sprinkle in the chopped coriander, mix well and place to one side ready to serve as required.

This works brilliantly when spread on a little bruschetta, or can even be used as a dip.

Super Simple Warm Pork Salsa

SERVES 2

- 2 rashers of bacon, diced
- 1 large tomato, finely diced
- ½ red onion, peeled and finely diced
- ½ red chilli, de-seeded and finely sliced
- ½ red pepper, de-seeded and finely diced

- Warm a frying pan on a medium heat and pour in a glug of olive oil. You may find it easier to cut the bacon with scissors rather than a knife, but once chopped, add in the bacon and cook for 30-60 seconds, stirring regularly.

- Next, add in the chopped tomato, onion, chilli and pepper, along with half a clove of freshly minced garlic. Stir the mixture in the pan well and cook for 3-4 minutes ,until the ingredients are beginning to soften.

- Stir in 1 tablespoon of tomato puree and a splash of balsamic vinegar.

- Remove from the pan and serve either as a dip or a topping.

This is a great salsa alternative to warm you up on cold days served simply on toasted bread.

Garlic and Green Pesto with Freshly Baked Bread

SERVES 2

- 1 tbsp green pesto
- A small pinch of freshly chopped mint
- A small pinch of freshly chopped oregano
- A splash of freshly squeezed lime juice
- 1 small, freshly baked baguette

● Spoon the green pesto into a small bowl. Add in a clove of freshly minced garlic and stir it into the pesto well.

● Add in the small pinch of mint and oregano, shortly followed by the freshly squeezed lime juice. Mix well together.

● Next, pour in some extra virgin olive oil. Pour in enough so that there is almost as much oil as the garlic and green pesto mixture - the oil should rise half a centimetre or so above the mixture. Of course, add less or more as you prefer. Stir well so the flavours season the oil then allow it to settle before serving.

● Slice the freshly baked bread and serve with the dip whilst still warm.

The longer you leave the pesto and oil to rest, the more the flavour comes through.

Sweet Tomato Dip and freshly baked Bread

- 150g/5oz cherry tomatoes, chopped
- 1 small strawberry, chopped
- A pinch of sugar
- A very small pinch of dried mixed herbs
- 1 small, freshly baked baguette

- Place the cherry tomatoes in a food processor, or use a hand blender and give a quick blast so they are relatively blended, but that a chunky textured mixture still exists. Alternatively, you can chop the tomatoes as finely as possible with a knife, repeatedly cutting back over them, and push into a bowl, gathering as much of the juices as possible.

- Chop a small strawberry as finely as possible, or use a pestle and mortar to mash the strawberry before adding into the tomato mixture. Add in a small pinch of sugar and a dash of dried mixed herbs.

- Add in a large glug of extra virgin olive oil, almost as much oil as mixture, and stir well. You can place to one side ready to serve along with freshly sliced warm crusty bread.

To reduce the sweetness, remove the strawberry, and store in the fridge for a while before serving for a lovely chilled dip to contrast the bread.

Wonderfully Easy Garlic Ciabatta

SERVES 2

- 1 fresh ciabatta
- 1 tbsp butter
- A pinch of dried mixed herbs
- A pinch of finely chopped fresh coriander
- A pinch of Parmesan, finely grated

● Pre-heat the grill to a medium heat.

● Cut the ciabatta in half lengthways, through the middle, as if making a sandwich. Separate the two halves.

● Mince a clove of garlic and mix it into the butter well. Spread the garlic butter over each half of the ciabatta – use less or more to your preference. Sprinkle across the mixed herbs and a little coriander to garnish, and top with a dusting of Parmesan cheese.

● Grill for 2-3 minutes, or until the butter has melted and the ciabatta is beginning to crisp on top. Grill for a little longer if you prefer crispier bread.

● Serve immediately.

Simply remove the Parmesan for a plain garlic ciabatta, or experiment with other Italian cheeses.

Italian Staple Tomato and Olive Oil Bruschetta

- 100g/3½oz cherry tomatoes, finely chopped
- ½ small red onion, peeled and finely chopped
- A pinch of ground paprika
- 2 large slices of toasted bruschetta
- Freshly chopped coriander to garnish

● Mash the cherry tomatoes so that a lumpy mixture is formed. Mix in the red onion along with a small clove, or half a regular clove, of freshly minced garlic. Season well with salt and pepper and add in a small pinch of paprika to bring a little heat to the mixture.

● Place the bruschetta slices on a plate to serve. Lightly drizzle some olive oil over them and then spoon the tomato and onion mixture on top.

● Garnish with a pinch of freshly chopped coriander and a drizzle of balsamic vinegar then enjoy.

Add a green or red chilli to give the flavour a more powerful kick, or a dash of sugar if you prefer a sweeter twist.

Lemon and Garlic Olives

SERVES 2

- ½ tsp lemon zest, finely grated
- A splash of freshly squeezed lemon juice
- A splash of apple cider vinegar
- ½ tsp parsley, freshly chopped
- 150g/5oz mixed olives

● Grate the lemon zest into a bowl and crush a small clove of garlic in with it too. Add a splash of lemon juice and a good splash of apple cider vinegar and mix well.

● Next, pour in a generous splash of olive oil and season well with salt and pepper. Sprinkle in the freshly chopped parsley and stir well.

● Add the olives, either still whole, or halved if you prefer, and gently mix the lemon and garlic oil over the olives so they are evenly covered. Serve with toothpicks for ease of eating.

Allow the excess oil to sit at the bottom of the bowl and use as a dip; use some deliciously warm bread to soak up the flavours.

Fresh Fig and Parma Ham Salad

SERVES 2

- 2 figs, quartered
- ½ lime, cut into wedges
- A pinch of freshly chopped basil
- 4 slices of Parma ham, torn or sliced
- A handful of fresh rocket leaves

● Place the chopped figs into a bowl. Gently squeeze the lime wedges so that a little juice begins to seep out, then add to the figs. Add in a splash of olive oil and season well with black pepper.

● Sprinkle in the freshly chopped basil leaves and give the mixture a gentle mix.

● Next, add in the torn Parma ham and toss well. Serve on a bed of fresh rocket leaves and top with a light splash of balsamic vinegar.

This makes an excellent platter when entertaining friends; simply increase the portions and serve on a large plate.

Salami and Fennel Raw Salad

- ½ tsp freshly squeezed lemon juice
- 1 tsp white wine vinegar
- A small drizzle of honey
- 1 fennel bulb, finely sliced
- 100g/3½oz thinly sliced salami

- Pour the freshly squeezed lemon juice into a bowl and add in the white wine vinegar and honey. Mix together to blend the ingredients and thin out the honey.

- Drizzle in a splash of olive oil and season well with salt and pepper.

- Mix everything together before adding in the finely sliced fennel. Toss the fennel in the dressing.

- Arrange the salami slices on a plate ready to serve, spoon the dressed fennel on top and enjoy.

Make this into a lunch by serving on top of a freshly toasted slice of bruschetta.

Aubergine and Courgette Salsa Stack

- ½ small aubergine, sliced
- ½ small courgette
- 2 large tomatoes, finely diced
- 1 tsp red onion, finely diced
- ½ tsp finely chopped parsley

● Pre-heat the oven to 400F/200C/Gas 4 and line a baking tray with grease-proof paper. Place the slices of aubergine and courgette on the tray and lightly brush with olive oil. Season with salt and pepper, then place in the over to cook for 4-5 minutes. Remove from the oven, turn the slices over, and return to the oven for a further 4-5 minutes.

● Meanwhile, place the finely diced tomatoes in a bowl, collecting as much of the juice as possible, and add in the red onion and parsley as well. Crush a clove of garlic into the mixture and drizzle in a little olive oil. Mix well and place to one side, ready to serve.

● Once tender, remove the aubergine and courgette slices from the oven and begin to stack on top of each other, alternating between the two vegetables, whilst spooning over the tomato salsa mixture, to create two vegetable towers (stack and serve on separate plates to serve 2 people). Serve immediately to enjoy whilst still warm.

This can make an excellent vegetarian main course accompanied with roasted vegetables and some grains.

Simply Italian Rocket and Prosciutto

- A large handful of rocket salad
- A splash of freshly squeezed lemon juice
- A dash of freshly squeezed lime juice
- 6 slices of prosciutto
- A small pinch of pine nuts (optional)

● Place a generous handful of rocket leaves in a bowl and drizzle over some extra virgin olive oil. Season well with freshly ground black pepper. Add in a good splash of lemon juice and a very small splash of lime juice. Toss the salad well to cover in the dressing.

● Spoon the dressed rocket onto a plate ready to serve. Fold and twist the prosciutto on top of the rocket salad and sprinkle over some pine nuts for texture if you so wish, or simply serve without.

A simple and classically Italian antipasti that is delicious and can be complemented by a small serving of olives.

Classic White Bean Soup

SERVES 2

- 75g/3oz tinned cannellini beans
- 750ml/1¼pint chicken stock
- ¼ onion, finely diced
- 60g/2½oz conchigliette
- 1 tsp Parmesan, finely grated

- On a medium heat, warm through the chicken stock and add in the cannellini beans. As these are already cooked, they will not take long to warm through. Crush a clove of garlic and add into the mixture along with the diced onion and a drizzle of olive oil.

- Once the stock and beans begin to simmer, briefly remove from the heat and use a hand blender, or pour into a food processor, to give the soup a good blast, blending most of the beans into the soup mixture to thicken. Do not worry if not all of the beans are blended down, as this will add texture.

- Return the mixture to the pan, stir well and return to the heat. Add in the conchigliette pasta to the soup and allow to cook for 10-12 minutes, or until cooked through and tender.

- Season well with salt and pepper and serve straight from the pan. Sprinkle some Parmesan on top to serve.

Serve with a homemade, or warmed through, crusty roll.

Raw Onion and Orange Salad

- 2 oranges, peeled and sliced
- ½ red onion, finely sliced
- 1 slice of onion, finely diced
- A large pinch of fresh parsley, finely chopped
- A pinch of orange zest, grated

- Place the sliced orange into a bowl and drizzle over extra virgin olive oil.

- Season with black pepper and add in the chopped onion. Mix well together so that the ingredients are coated in the seasoned oil dressing.

- Add in the freshly chopped parsley and orange zest then toss the salad mixture once more before serving.

Like most raw salad, this is best served chilled; prepare in advance and store in the fridge for a nice fresh, crisp texture and taste.

As-Italian-As-It-Gets Tomato and Mozzarella Salad

- 150g/5oz buffalo mozzarella, drained and sliced
- 4 large tomatoes, sliced
- A handful of fresh basil leaves
- A small pinch of dried oregano
- A small pinch of dried basil

- Simply place the sliced mozzarella and the sliced tomatoes in separate piles to one side, ready to arrange.

- On a plate, begin to arrange the cheese and tomato by placing one slice of mozzarella on top of a slice of tomato, overlapping it, and repeating this process alternating between the two to create an aesthetic red and white pattern around the edge of the plate. Fill the gap in the middle using mozzarella and tomato slices arranged in a similar fashion.

- Drizzle a little splash of olive oil over, but not too much. Scatter across some fresh basil leaves and the tiniest of sprinklings of dried oregano, basil and black pepper to season.

Add a drizzle of balsamic vinegar on top to finish this truly traditional Italian dish.

Anchovy, Olive and Tomato Medley

- 25g/1oz tinned anchovies
- 50g/2oz mixed pitted olives
- 25g/1oz sundried tomatoes
- A pinch of orange zest, grated
- A pinch of fresh parsley, finely chopped

- Drain the tinned anchovies and place into a bowl.

- Drain the olives and sundried tomatoes, if also tinned, and add to the same bowl as the anchovies, tossing together well. The natural oils from the preserves should be sufficient, but if not, add a drizzle of olive oil.

- Crush a small clove of garlic and add to the medley, stirring well. Grate some orange zest in, along with the freshly chopped parsley.

- Toss the medley together well once more then serve.

Bursting with flavours and richness, this is a deliciously classic Italian medley and complements a cold glass of white wine beautifully.

Tomato and Olive Salad

- ¼ tsp freshly squeezed lemon juice
- 4 large tomatoes, chopped
- 75g/3oz pitted olives
- 50g/2oz cucumber, chopped
- 1 tbsp red wine vinegar

● Pour the lemon juice into a small bowl and mix with some olive oil. Season with salt and pepper to form a light dressing.

● Place the chopped tomatoes, olives and cucumber in a bowl and toss together well. Drizzle over the prepared dressing, along with the red wine vinegar and a drizzle of balsamic vinegar.

● Toss once more and serve.

This is a deliciously simple salad and the cucumber adds a freshness to the oil-based recipe.

Leek and Pepper Vinaigrette Salad

- 1 large leek, chopped
- 100g/3½oz red, yellow and green bell peppers, de-seeded and sliced
- 25g/1oz red onion, sliced
- 1 tsp freshly chopped parsley
- 1 tsp freshly squeezed lemon juice

● Pre-heat the oven to 180C/350F/Gas 4 and bring a pan of water to boil. Add the chopped leek to the pan and boil for 5-7 minutes so the leek begins to soften. Drain and place in a small roasting dish.

● Add in the sliced peppers and onion and drizzle over some olive oil. Mince a small clove of garlic and season well with salt and pepper. Stir the leeks, peppers and onion so they are mixed and covered well in the oil and garlic seasoning. Sprinkle over the parsley and lemon juice and toss once more.

● Place in the oven and roast for 10-12 minutes, or until it begins to soften but not crisp. Remove from the oven and serve, ensuring that you pour all juices from the dish over the warm salad.

● Drizzle over a little balsamic vinegar and serve.

This makes a wonderful starter or snack and can be used as a side dish with fresh fish as it compliments beautifully.

Sundried Tomato and Mozzarella Rocket Salad

- Two large handfuls of fresh rocket leaves
- 40g/1½oz sundried tomatoes
- 100g/3½oz mozzarella, sliced
- 1 tsp green pesto
- A large handful of fresh basil leaves

- Place the fresh rocket leaves into a bowl and add in the sundried tomatoes.

- Depending on the size of the tomatoes you may wish to chop them, alternatively, leave them whole. Add in the mozzarella, either sliced or torn to your preference, and toss the ingredients well together.

- Drizzle in a splash of olive oil, a splash of balsamic vinegar, green pesto and ½ clove of fresh, crushed garlic.

- Gently stir the salad well to evenly coat it as much as possible. Tear up the basil leaves and sprinkle on top to serve.

This delicious salad is quick & easy and benefits from the fresh peppery flavour of the rocket leaves; add in some chicken or pancetta for extra protein.

nom nom ITALY

carne e pesce

Grilled Tuna Steak and Three Bean Salad

- 1 fresh tuna steak
- 25g/1oz tinned white beans
- 25g/1oz tinned red kidney beans
- 25g/1oz tinned lima beans
- ½ small red onion, peeled and finely diced

● Pre-heat the grill to a medium heat and brush the tuna steak with some olive oil. Season with a little black pepper and place under the grill for 2-3 minutes, or until the tuna begins to brown. Turn the steak over and repeat on the other side. Adjust the cooking time depending on how you prefer your steak to be cooked.

● Meanwhile, drain the tinned beans and place in a bowl along with the finely chopped red onion. Add in a drizzle of olive oil and mince a clove of garlic into the bean mixture. Place a frying pan on a medium heat and add the beans and onion to the pan. Warm them through, add in 2 tablespoons of tomato puree and season well with salt and pepper.

● Spoon the beans into the centre of a plate or bowl and place the cooked tuna steak on top. Drizzle over a splash of balsamic vinegar and serve.

Add a little baby leaf or rocket salad to complement the bean salad.

Garlic and Fennel Pork

SERVES 2

- 250g/9oz diced pork
- 1 red chilli, de-seeded and finely sliced
- ½ fennel bulb, sliced
- 150g/5oz tinned tomatoes with herbs
- 2 sprigs of fresh basil

- Pre-heat the oven to 350F /180C/Gas 4.

- Warm a good glug of olive oil in a frying pan. Mince 2 cloves of garlic and add into the pan. Cook for 30-60 seconds then add in the diced pork, chilli and fennel slices. Move the ingredients around the pan and cook for as long as it takes to seal/brown the pork, but not cook through.

- Pour the tinned tomatoes into a small dish and add in the contents of the pan. Add in the basil sprigs and either cover with a lid or with foil. Place in the oven for 25-30 minutes.

- Remove from the oven and serve with your choice of accompaniment.

This works brilliantly with creamed potatoes or rice.

Tomato and Parmesan Frittata

- 1 onion, peeled and finely chopped
- 2 medium tomatoes, chopped
- 3 large eggs
- 40g/1½oz Parmesan, grated
- 1 tsp freshly chopped parsley

- Place a frying pan on a medium heat and drizzle in a teaspoon of olive oil. Add in the onions and sauté for 3-4 minutes, stirring occasionally, so they begin to turn a golden brown in colour and soften. Add in ½ a small clove of garlic, minced, and the chopped tomatoes then sauté for another minute or two.

- In a small bowl, whisk the eggs together, season well with salt and pepper and sprinkle in the cheese and parsley. Drain any excess water or oil from the tomato and onion mixture in the pan, and empty the contents into the egg mixture. Return the pan to the heat, but reduce the temperature, and pour in the tomato, onion and egg mixture.

- While the frittata begins to cook through and set, turn on the grill to warm up. Once the frittata has set in the pan, it is likely to be a little runny on top; place the pan under the grill to allow the egg to fully cook and crisp lightly on top.

- Once cooked, remove from the grill. Cut into slices and either serve warm or enjoy cooled.

Serve with a freshly prepared salad.

Monkfish with Tomato and Anchovy Sauce

- 1 tsp freshly squeezed lemon juice
- 1 tsp freshly chopped parsley
- 2 fresh monkfish steaks
- 350g/12oz tinned tomatoes with mixed herbs
- 50g/2oz tinned anchovies, chopped

● Pour the lemon juice into a bowl and sprinkle in the parsley. Add in 2-3 tablespoons of olive oil, depending on the size of your monkfish steaks, and combine well. Place the monkfish steaks in the lemon and parsley oil and allow to marinate for 1-2 hours.

● Place a deep pan on a medium heat and add in the monkfish steaks. Simply remove the steaks from the bowl and put in the pan; do not pour in the excess lemon and parsley oil. Cook the fish steaks until you can see it whitening through then turn over to finish cooking through the other side.

● Meanwhile, warm the tinned chopped tomatoes in another pan. Mince 2 cloves of garlic and add in with a generous seasoning of salt and pepper. Spoon in 1 tablespoon of tomato puree to help the sauce thicken. Allow the sauce to simmer and reduce slightly. Add in the chopped anchovies, stir and simmer for a further 2-3 minutes.

● Once the fish is cooked, serve immediately onto a plate and pour over the tomato and anchovy sauce.

This can be simply enjoyed with a bed of fresh salad leaves or with some crispy potatoes.

Rosemary and Garlic Oven Baked Trout

- ½ onion, finely chopped
- ½ courgette, finely diced
- 4 sprigs of rosemary
- A large splash of dry white wine
- 2 fresh whole trout

● Pre-heat the oven to 350°F/180C/Gas 4. Meanwhile, place a frying pan on a medium heat and drizzle in a generous splash of olive oil. Mince 2 large cloves of garlic and add to the pan along with the onion and courgette. Sauté for 1-2 minutes and then add in the rosemary and dry white wine. Allow the mixture to simmer for 2-3 minutes.

● Cut two large squares of baking parchment, big enough to fold over and cover/wrap the trout entirely. Spoon some of the mixture from the pan onto each of the pieces of paper and spread it out with the back of a spoon to create a bed for the trout to rest on. Lay the trout on top and spoon over the remaining mixture and rosemary sprigs. Fold the paper over so that the trout is covered then bake in the oven for 17-20 minutes, or until the trout is cooked through and beginning to turn golden.

● Remove from the oven and serve immediately, spooning any remaining garlic, rosemary, onion and courgette mixture over the top for added flavour.

Serve with some crushed new potatoes or a fresh tomato salad.

Grilled Garlic and Lemon Swordfish

SERVES 2

- Juice of 1 lemon
- 2 swordfish steaks
- A large splash of dry white wine
- 1 sprig of oregano, roughly chopped

- Squeeze the lemon juice into a bowl and stir in 2 tablespoons of olive oil. Pour in a splash of white wine and lightly season with salt and pepper. Stir in one clove of garlic, minced, as well as the chopped oregano, and then put the sauce to one side.

- Season your swordfish and then add to a very hot, lightly oiled griddle pan. Cook the steak for around 2 minutes on each side, or a little longer if you prefer it not to be pink in the middle. Once cooked, place the swordfish steaks onto your plates and ladle the sauce over the top, ready to serve.

Swap the oregano with parsley if you prefer and serve with steamed seasonal greens.

Turkey and Mozzarella Stuffed Peppers

- 1 onion, chopped finely
- 200/7oz cauliflower rice
- 200g/7oz ground turkey
- 2 bell peppers
- 100g/3½oz mozzarella, torn

- Preheat the oven to 350°F/180C/Gas 4. Place a frying pan on a medium heat and add in a good glug of olive oil. Add in the onion, cauliflower rice and a large clove of minced garlic, sauté for 2-3 minutes.

- Add the ground turkey into pan, seasoning with salt and pepper to taste, and keep stirring until the meat is cooked through. Meanwhile, slice off the tops of the peppers and remove the seeds inside.

- Once the meat is cooked, place the peppers into a casserole dish, fill each one with a quarter of the meat mixture and top with shreds of mozzarella. Cover each pepper in aluminium foil and cook for around 40 minutes.

- Remove the stuffed peppers from the oven and carefully remove the tin foil. Return them to the oven for a further 5-7 minutes to soften a little more and begin to crisp slightly.

These peppers are great served with a drizzle of marinara sauce and fresh salad.

Meat-Free Marinara Meatballs

- 1 small onion, peeled and finely chopped
- 400g/14oz tinned plum tomatoes, chopped
- 200g/7oz Quorn mince
- 50g/2oz breadcrumbs
- 1 egg

- First, prepare the marinara sauce. Place the chopped onion with a large clove of garlic, minced, in a pan with a good splash of olive oil. Cook, stirring continuously, for 2-3 minutes or until soft. Add in the chopped plum tomatoes and parsley and season with salt and pepper. Allow the mixture to simmer for 7-10 minutes.

- Meanwhile, prepare the meatballs by combing the Quorn mince, breadcrumbs and egg, along with a minced small clove of garlic in a large bowl. Mix well and roll the mixture around with your hands, compacting it, and then eventually dividing into 8-12 balls, depending on how big you would like them.

- Next, add the meatballs into the pan containing the marinara sauce and allow to simmer for around 30 more minutes. Once cooked, divide the meatballs and sauce between your serving plates and enjoy.

This tastes great with a dusting of Parmesan and is excellent served with spaghetti.

Sundried Tomato Stuffed Chicken Breasts

- 100g/3½oz low-fat soft cheese
- 2 tbsp sundried tomatoes
- ½ sprig parsley, finely chopped
- 2 chicken breasts
- 2 tomatoes, sliced

● Pre-heat the oven to 400F/200C/Gas 6. In a bowl, combine the soft cheese and sundried tomatoes along with a minced clove of garlic, the freshly chopped parsley and a good pinch of salt and pepper.

● Next, take each chicken breast and cut a slit along the side, which can be opened out into a pocket using your knife. Spoon in half of the soft cheese and tomato mixture into each chicken breast, pressing down to close.

● Place the stuffed chicken onto a baking tray and add the sliced tomato slices on top. Drizzle over a small splash of olive oil and roast for 20 minutes until golden.

● Serve straight from the oven.

Best served with steamed vegetables or salad; for a juicier breast, wrap the fillets in tinfoil to cook.

Breadcrumb and Parmesan Aubergine

- 125g/4oz breadcrumbs
- A large pinch of freshly chopped oregano
- 200g/7oz tinned chopped tomatoes
- 2 small aubergines, halved lengthways
- 175g/6oz Parmesan, grated

- Pre-heat the oven to 400F/200C/Gas6. In a bowl, mix the breadcrumbs with a pinch of salt and half a tbsp of olive oil. Use your hands to combine the ingredients together well and then place to one side. Next, place an ovenproof pan on a medium heat with a good splash of olive oil. Add one minced clove of garlic, the oregano and seasoning. Sauté for around 30 secs before stirring in the chopped tomatoes. Simmer for 5 minutes until the sauce begins to thicken.

- Meanwhile, place the **aubergines** in a large bowl. Rub some olive oil and seasoning into the eggplant. Once the sauce is ready, place the eggplant halves cut-side down into the pan and place in the oven for 20 to 25 minutes, or until the tops look puckered.

- Remove the pan from the oven and flip the **aubergine** halves so that the cut sides are facing up, then splash some of the sauce over the **aubergines** and top evenly with the breadcrumbs and grated Parmesan. Place the pan back into the oven for a further 4 minutes until the breadcrumbs turn golden brown.

- To serve, divide the **aubergines** evenly between serving plates and dress with chopped oregano.

Guazzetto Prawns with Chickpeas and Chilli

- ½ tsp. chilli flakes
- ½ red chilli, de-seeded and finely sliced
- A large pinch of freshly chopped rosemary
- 150g/5oz chickpeas, cooked and drained
- 300g/11oz fresh medium prawns, peeled

● Place a pan on a medium heat and add in a good glug of olive oil. Mince a large clove of garlic and add into the pan with the chilli flakes, sliced chilli, chopped rosemary, and a heaped tablespoon of tomato puree. Allow the ingredients to simmer for 2-3 minutes, regularly stirring.

● Next, add in the chickpeas and season with a pinch of salt and pepper. Allow the mixture to cook for a few more minutes, then add the peeled prawns to the sauce and simmer for 3-4 minutes, or until the prawns are coloured.

● Remove from the heat and divide evenly between plates, serving with a drizzle of olive oil and some chopped rosemary.

This dish is delicious when served with freshly baked bread.

Lamb and Watercress Salad

- A large pinch of freshly chopped rosemary
- 2 thick boneless lamb leg steaks
- 125g/4oz baby plum tomatoes, chopped
- 75g/3oz watercress, stems removed
- 50g/2oz feta, crumbled

● Rub the fresh rosemary and a good splash of olive oil over the lamb steaks to season. Place the steaks in a small dish, along with some peeled garlic, and allow to marinate at room temperature for 30-60 minutes.

● Heat a frying pan over a high heat and add in the lamb steaks and tomatoes to the pan. Sear the meat for around 2 minutes on each side until golden, or for a little longer if you prefer it more well done. Remove the lamb and tomatoes and put to one side to rest.

● Next, take the pan off the heat and pour in a tablespoon of balsamic vinegar and a tablespoon of olive oil, as well as any juices from the lamb, whisking together to make a dressing.

● Take the lamb and slice it thickly before adding it to your serving plates on a bed of watercress and tomatoes. To serve, crumble feta over the plate and spoon on the dressing.

The longer you leave the steaks to marinate, the more intense the flavour.

Wonderfully Simple Bean Casserole

SERVES 2

- 2 carrots, peeled and chopped
- 350g/12oz tinned chopped tomatoes
- 200ml/7floz vegetable stock
- 100g/3½oz tinned cannellini beans, drained and rinsed
- 100g/3½oz tinned borlotti beans, drained and rinsed

- In a large casserole pan, heat a good glug of olive oil over a medium heat. Add in the carrots and sauté for 7-8 minutes, stirring regularly.

- Next, stir in a minced clove of garlic and the tomatoes, followed by the vegetable stock made with boiling water. Season well, add salt and pepper and let it simmer for 30 minutes until the liquid has thickened.

- When the vegetables are tender, mix in the beans for 5 minutes and remove from heat. To serve, spoon the bean casserole into serving dishes.

A garnish of oregano can add some excellent flavour to this dish, or can even be added in during the cooking process.

Red-Wine Roasted Duck

SERVES 4

- 2 duck legs
- 200g/7oz tinned chopped tomatoes
- 125ml/4floz red wine
- 250ml/8½floz boiling chicken stock
- ½ red onion, finely diced

- Pre-heat the oven to 400F/200C/Gas 6. Season each duck leg with a good rub of salt and black pepper, massaging it into the meat with a light brushing of olive oil.

- Roast the duck legs in a large pan in the oven for around 35-45 minutes, depending on the size of the leg, or until browned and cooked through.

- Meanwhile, pour a good glug of olive oil into a pan over a medium heat and add in the onions, allowing them to soften. Next, add in two cloves of crushed garlic, a heaped tablespoon of tomato puree and good pinch of salt and pepper to season. Stir the mixture well for 30 seconds. Pour in the red wine and chopped tomatoes and allow the sauce to simmer for 4-5 minutes until it thickens slightly and reduces. Pour in the stock, stir well and simmer for a further few minutes.

- Once cooked, pour off any accumulated fat from the duck leg pan and add the legs to the sauce. Reduce the heat to a gentle simmer and cook until the meat is tender, usually around 45 minutes. Skim off any fat and transfer the duck legs to a baking dish. Pour the sauce over the meat and bake for around 30 minutes until the legs have browned on top. Divide evenly onto serving dishes.

Pour and skim off the excess fat from the duck.

Chorizo and Chicken Bake

- 50g/2oz chorizo, diced
- 2 skinless chicken breasts, diced
- 1 large sweet potato, peeled and cubed
- 1 red onion, roughly chopped
- 150ml/5floz chicken stock

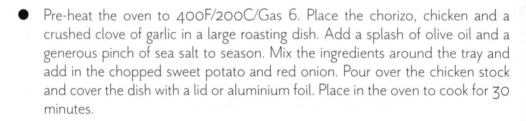

● Pre-heat the oven to 400F/200C/Gas 6. Place the chorizo, chicken and a crushed clove of garlic in a large roasting dish. Add a splash of olive oil and a generous pinch of sea salt to season. Mix the ingredients around the tray and add in the chopped sweet potato and red onion. Pour over the chicken stock and cover the dish with a lid or aluminium foil. Place in the oven to cook for 30 minutes.

● Remove the lid or foil, stir and return to the oven for a further 15-20 minutes to allow the chicken to cook through and become golden.

● Remove from the oven and serve straight from the dish, spooning over the juices from the pan to add flavour and moisture.

Add in a red chilli for a fiery twist, or a handful of green beans for a balanced side.

Italian Baked Cod

- 1 onion, finely chopped
- 200g/7oz tinned chopped tomatoes with herbs
- 2 cod fillets, skin and bones removed
- A handful of mixed pitted olives
- 50g/2oz spinach

- Preheat the oven to 350F/180C/Gas 4. In a large frying pan, heat a large splash of olive oil on a medium heat and sauté the onions until softened. Crush a large clove of garlic and add to the pan. Sauté for a further minute, pour in the chopped tomatoes, and season with salt and pepper. Simmer for 12-15 minutes, stirring occasionally.

- Next, add the olives and spinach and simmer for a further 10 minutes to thicken the sauce.

- Place the cod in a shallow baking tray and season with salt and pepper. Then evenly spoon the sauce onto each piece of cod, arranging the olives on top. Cover the dish with aluminium foil and bake for 25 minutes, or slightly longer for thicker pieces of cod.

- To serve, place a piece of cod onto each serving plate and spoon over any remaining sauce.

For added texture, crush a handful of pine nuts and add into the mixture to cover the cod.

Sizzling Sirloin with Garlic Mushrooms and Tomatoes

- 50g/2oz cherry tomatoes, chopped
- 50g/2oz mushrooms, chopped
- A pinch of dried oregano
- A pinch of dried parsley
- 1 fresh free-range, good quality sirloin steak

- Warm one teaspoon of olive oil in a pan and add in the cherry tomatoes and mushrooms.

- Sauté the ingredients well for a minute or two. Crush a clove of fresh garlic and add to the pan along with the oregano and parsley.

- Stir well and cook for a further 3-4 minutes, or until the mushrooms and tomatoes are beginning to soften and turn golden brown.

- Meanwhile, put a separate frying pan on a high heat. Brush the steak with oil and season the steak well with salt and pepper.

- Cook the steak for 1-2 minutes on each side, or for longer depending on how well done you like your steak.

- Serve the steak on a plate with the garlic mushroom and tomato mixture and immediately enjoy.

Add a small portion of chips or garlic ciabatta for a carbohydrate boost.

Pesto and Mozzarella Stuffed Chicken

SERVES 1

- 1 large chicken fillet breast
- 1 tbsp green pesto
- 2 mini mozzarella balls
- 1 slice of Parma ham
- 2 tsp of Parmesan cheese

- Pre-heat the oven to 350F/180c/Gas4.

- Slice the chicken breast along its side; not completely in half, but so that a pocket is created in which to add a pesto and mozzarella stuffing.

- Spoon in the green pesto and spread around the pocket to cover the chicken breast well inside. Place the 2 mini mozzarella balls inside the pocket and push the fillet back together.

- Wrap the fillet in the slice of Parma ham and sprinkle over a good pinch of Parmesan cheese to create a nice cheesy crisp.

- Place in the oven for 30-35 minutes, or until the chicken is thoroughly cooked through. Serve with your choice of accompaniments.

The history of Parma ham dates back to ancient Roman times when Cato the "Censor" first cited the extraordinary flavour of the air-cured ham made in the town of Parma.

Beef Fillet in Laurel Wreath

- 1 free-range, good quality fillet of beef
- 1 tsp mustard
- 2-3 fresh whole bay leaves
- 1 tsp crushed black peppercorns
- 25ml/1floz Italian brandy
-

● Pre-heat the oven to 275F/140C/Gas 1.

● Season the beef fillet lightly with salt and pepper. Smear the mustard over the fillet to thinly cover the meat.

● Place a pan on a medium heat and add in a dash of olive oil. Place the fillet into the pan and quickly seal the steak, browning it on all sides. Once completely and evenly browned carefully wrap the bay leaves around the fillet steak; how many you will need will depend on the actual size of the fillet to roughly cover the outside edge (use cooking twine to hold them in place). Then place the steak in the oven for 10-15 minutes.

● Meanwhile, a few minutes before removing the fillet from the oven, drain any excess juices from the frying pan and add in the crushed peppercorns and Italian brandy. Return the pan to the heat and warm through the sauce. Remove from the fillet from the oven and serve on a warmed plate. Drizzle over the Italian brandy sauce and serve immediately with your choice of sides.

For a distinctive character, try using Vecchia Romagna - one of the finest brandies worldwide.

nom
nom
ITALY
pasta

Chilli and Tomato Farfalle

SERVES 2

- 200g /7oz farfalle pasta
- 100g/3½oz cherry tomatoes, chopped
- 1 small red chilli, de-seeded and finely sliced
- 100g/3½oz passata
- ½ tsp chilli flakes

- Bring a pan of water to boil. Add in the farfalle along with a small pinch of salt and cook for 10-12 minutes, stirring every few minutes.

- Meanwhile, warm a saucepan to a medium heat and drizzle in some olive oil. Once the oil is warmed through, add in some freshly minced garlic, the chopped tomatoes and red chilli. Simmer for 2-3 minutes, stirring regularly. Pour in the passata, stirring well, and 1 tbsp tomato puree, blending it into the tomato mixture.

- Sprinkle in the chilli flakes and allow the mixture to simmer for a further 2-3 minutes, stirring every now and then to ensure it does not burn or stick to the pan.

- Once cooked, drain the pasta and place in a bowl or on a plate to serve. Pour over the chilli tomato sauce and serve.

Garnish with fresh basil to serve.

Classically Simple Penne Arrabbiata

SERVES 2

- 200g/7oz penne pasta
- 1 red chilli, de-seeded and finely sliced
- 350g/12oz tinned chopped tomatoes
- A handful of fresh basil leaves
- Parmesan to serve

- Bring a pan of water to boil. Place the penne into the water and add a small pinch of salt. Cook for 10-12 minutes, stirring occasionally.

- Meanwhile, place a saucepan on a medium heat and drizzle in some olive oil. Once the oil is warmed through add in one clove of freshly minced garlic along with the red chilli and cook for 1-2 minutes, stirring regularly to avoid either ingredient burning or sticking to the pan.

- Add in the chopped tomatoes and reduce the heat slightly. Tear the basil leaves and add them into the arrabbiata mixture. Stir well and allow the mixture to simmer for 4-5 minutes or until it has thickened slightly. Stir occasionally to prevent the sauce from burning.

- Once cooked through, drain the penne and return to the saucepan. Pour in the arrabbiata sauce and mix well. Serve straight from the pan. Add any leftover basil leaves on top to serve along with finely chopped or grated Parmesan.

This is a super simple Italian classic that can be whipped up from basic store cupboard essentials.

Mild and Creamy Arrabbiata Twist

- 200g/7oz fusilli pasta
- 350g/12oz tinned chopped tomatoes
- ½ tsp mild chilli powder
- A small handful of fresh basil leaves

● Bring a pan of water to boil and add in the fusilli with a small pinch of salt. Cook for 10-12 minutes, stirring occasionally.

● While the pasta cooks, warm a dash of olive in a saucepan on a medium heat. Add in half a clove of freshly minced garlic and cook for 1 minute, stirring regularly, before adding in the chopped tomatoes, tomato puree and mild chilli powder. Tear the basil leaves and add them into the mixture too, stirring well. Stir the mixture well and allow to simmer for 3-4 minutes.

● Once the fusilli is cooked through, drain the pasta and return it to the saucepan. Pour in the tomato sauce from the pan and mix with the pasta so it is evenly covered. Spoon in the crème fraiche, stir well into the sauce and allow the mixture to warm through.

● Serve straight from the pan.

A wonderful twist on a traditional Arrabbiata sauce that is a little gentler on the taste buds.

Mushroom and Garlic Pappardelle

- 200g/7oz pappardelle pasta
- 200g/7oz button mushrooms, chopped
- 50g/2oz spinach
- 1 tbsp Parmesan, grated
- 2 tbsp double cream

- Bring a pan of water to boil. Add in the pappardelle and a pinch of salt. Cook for 10-12 minutes or until thoroughly cooked through.

- Place a saucepan on a medium heat and drizzle in some olive oil. Mince two cloves of garlic and add to the pan with the chopped button mushrooms. Cook for 2-3 minutes until the mushrooms are golden and softened.

- Add in the spinach, stirring well, and cook for a further minute so the spinach begins to soften and wilt. Season with black pepper and sprinkle in the Parmesan. Once the cheese has almost completely melted, pour in the double cream and mix well, reducing the heat slightly but allowing the mixture to warm through.

- Once cooked through, remove the pasta from the heat and drain. Spoon the pasta into the pan of sauce and mix well, or if there is not enough room, return the pasta to the saucepan and pour the creamy garlic and mushroom sauce into the saucepan, mixing well.

- Serve immediately.

White Wine and Garlic Linguine

SERVES 2

- 175g/6oz linguine
- 50g/2oz mushrooms, chopped
- 100ml/3½floz dry white wine
- 3 tbsp crème fraiche

- Bring a pan of water to boil. Add in the linguine along with a pinch of salt. Cook for 10-12 minutes until soft and cooked through.

- Place a saucepan on a medium heat and drizzle in a teaspoon of olive oil. Crush two cloves of garlic into the pan along with the chopped mushrooms. Season with salt and pepper and allow to cook for 2-3 minutes so the mushrooms begin to soften. Pour in the white wine and stir well. Reduce the heat slightly and simmer for 5-7 minutes, stirring occasionally to prevent burning, allow some of the wine to steam off slightly.

- Once the wine has reduced, and the pasta is cooked through and ready, spoon in the crème fraiche, stirring well. Drain the pasta and serve in a bowl or on a plate.

- Pour the creamy white wine sauce on top and serve.

If you have the time, allowing the wine to simmer for longer adds even more flavour.

Homemade Green Pesto Pasta

SERVES 2

- 200g/7oz wholegrain spaghetti
- 1 large bunch of fresh basil
- 40g/1½oz pine nuts
- 40g/1½oz Parmesan, grated
- A splash of freshly squeezed lemon juice

- Bring a pan of water to boil and cook the spaghetti for 10 minutes, or until cooked through and tender.

- Meanwhile, prepare the pesto sauce. Tear the basil leaves off all of the stems and tear them up. Place them in a food processor along with 2 cloves of freshly minced garlic and 125ml/4floz of extra virgin olive oil. Give the mixture a good pulse to blend and then add in the pine nuts, Parmesan and a good splash of freshly squeezed lemon juice, before pulsing the mixture until a smooth, combined sauce is created.

- Once cooked, drain the spaghetti and return to the saucepan. Spoon in the green pesto sauce and mix well to cover the spaghetti. Return to the heat, stirring continuously to prevent sticking, and allow the pesto pasta to warm through.

- Serve immediately, and if you have any Parmesan leftover, grate a little on top to garnish.

This is so simple to make and can be easily stored for lunch the following day.

Quick and Easy Pesto, Caper and Tomato Pasta

- 200g/7oz fresh fusilli pasta
- 100g/3½oz green pesto
- 75g/3oz cherry tomatoes, halved
- 1 tbsp tinned or jarred capers
- 50g/2oz Parmesan cheese, thinly sliced

- Bring a pan of water to boil. Add in the fresh fusilli and cook for 3 minutes, or longer if otherwise instructed.

- Drain the pasta and return it to the pan. Spoon in the ready-made green pesto and mix thoroughly. Add in the cherry tomatoes and capers, then warm through on a low heat. Not pre-cooking the tomatoes adds texture to the pasta, however if you prefer a softer skin you can either quickly fry them in a pan with some olive oil, or grill them, before adding to the pasta.

- Once the pesto sauce, tomato and pasta mixture is warmed through, add in the sliced Parmesan and give everything a quick stir before serving. Try not to allow the Parmesan to melt too much in the pan so you get a nice cheesy crunch.

Pesto originated in Genoa around the 16th century and traditionally consists of crushed garlic, basil and pine nuts blended with Parmesan cheese and olive oil.

Fiery Tomato and Tuna Tagliatelle

- 175g/6oz tagliatelle
- 200g/7oz tinned chopped tomatoes with chilli
- 1 small red chilli, de-seeded and finely sliced
- ½ tsp ground paprika
- 60g/2½oz tinned tuna in brine

- Bring a saucepan of water to boil and add in the tagliatelle along with a pinch of salt. Cook for 12 minutes, or until tender.

- While the pasta cooks, warm a frying pan on a medium heat and add a small splash of olive oil. Pour in the tinned tomatoes, chilli and paprika and simmer for 2-3 minutes, stirring regularly. Stir in a tablespoon of tomato puree and allow the sauce to simmer for a further 30-60 seconds. Drain the tuna and add into the chilli tomato sauce. Keep stirring and allow the tuna to warm through in the sauce.

- Once cooked, drain the tagliatelle and spoon into a bowl to serve. Pour the chilli, tomato and tuna sauce on top and serve.

Garnish with fresh coriander and increase or decrease the amount of chilli as desired.

Deliciously Italian Olive Conchiglie

SERVES 2

- 200/7oz conchiglie
- 75g/3oz pitted olives, halved
- 1 tbsp tinned or jarred capers
- 1½ tbsp dry white wine
- 1 tbsp crème fraiche

● Bring a pan of water to boil. Add in the conchiglie to the water, with a little salt, and cook for 10-12 minutes or until cooked through.

● Meanwhile, in a saucepan, heat a good splash of olive oil on a medium heat. Add in the olives and cook for 2-3 minutes, turning them regularly. Once the skins begin to soften, add in the capers as well as a large clove of freshly minced garlic, shortly followed by the white wine. Allow the olives, garlic and capers to simmer in the wine for a further 2 minutes. The wine should begin to steam off; if most of the wine is still present, reduce the heat slightly and allow the mixture to simmer for a further minute or two. Finally, spoon in the crème fraiche and stir well.

● Drain the pasta and serve straight onto a plate or into a bowl. Spoon the olive, caper and cream sauce over the conchiglie and enjoy whilst hot.

Garnish with some freshly torn basil and a sprinkling of Parmesan.

Pork Lardons and Red Pesto Farfalle

- 200g/7oz farfalle pasta
- 100g/3½oz bacon lardons
- 100g/3½oz red pesto sauce
- A large handful of freshly torn basil leaves
- 50g/2oz Parmesan cheese, finely grated

- Bring a pan of water to boil. Add in a small drizzle of olive oil and the farfalle. Cook for 10-12 minutes, or until cooked through and tender.

- While the farfalle cooks, place a pan on a medium heat and add a good splash of olive oil. Add in the bacon lardons and cook for 4-5 minutes, stirring regularly. Once cooked through and beginning to crisp, remove the lardons from the heat and place to one side while you drain the farfalle.

- Once drained, return the pasta to the saucepan and spoon in the lardons. Try to avoid too much oil or juices from the pan spilling into the pasta as this could make the sauce a little too oily.

- Spoon in the red pesto sauce and throw in the torn basil leaves. Return to the heat and warm the pesto sauce through.

- Remove from the heat and serve with the grated Parmesan on top.

As a lighter lunch, reduce the measurements proportionately and serve on a bed of fresh rocket leaves.

Warm Pasta Salad

SERVES 2

- 200g/7oz farfalle pasta
- 2 spring onions, finely sliced
- 4 sundried tomatoes, chopped
- ½ tsp Dijon mustard
- A handful of rocket leaves

● Bring a pan of water to boil. Add in the farfalle and cook for 10-12 minutes, or until tender.

● Meanwhile, begin to prepare the other ingredients. Place the chopped spring onions and sundried tomatoes in a bowl and add a drizzle of olive oil. Mince a clove of garlic and add into the mixture. Spoon in the Dijon mustard and mix well. Roughly chop up the rocket leaves and add to the spring onion and tomato mixture, stirring well once more. Season with salt and pepper and place to one side.

● Once cooked, drain the pasta and then return to the pan. Spoon over the tomato, spring onion and rocket dressing and mix well so the farfalle is evenly coated in the mixture. Return to the pan and warm through, continuously stirring, then serve.

This is wonderful to enjoy warm and equally great once cooled for lunch the next day.

Family Friendly Sausage Pasta Bake

SERVES 4

- 5 pork sausages
- 400g/14oz fusilli pasta
- 400g/14oz tinned chopped tomatoes
- 2 tbsp crème fraiche
- 75g/3oz mature cheddar cheese, grated

- Pre-heat a grill to a medium heat. Cook the sausages under the grill for 10-12 minutes, turning the sausages every few minutes to ensure the cook evenly.

- Meanwhile, bring a pan of water to boil and add in the fusilli pasta with a pinch of salt. Cook for 12 minutes and then drain.

- Once cooked through, chop the sausages into slices and place, with the drained fusilli, into the saucepan used to cook the pasta. Add in the tin of chopped tomatoes, a crushed clove of garlic and season with salt and pepper. Warm through on a low heat while you pre-heat the oven to 350F (gas 4).

- Spoon in the crème fraiche and mix well until a pinky/orange pasta sauce is created. Stir some of the cheddar into the pasta and sauce and save the rest to sprinkle on top. Spoon the pasta into a baking dish and sprinkle over the remaining cheese.

- Place in the oven and cook for 15-20 minutes, or a little longer if you prefer a crispier topping. Best served straight from the oven.

A true family favourite; serve with a fresh salad or chunky garlic ciabatta.

Super Simple Homemade Spaghetti Bolognese

SERVES 2

- 200g/7oz spaghetti
- 125g/4oz minced beef
- ½ onion, finely chopped
- 1 carrot, peeled and finely diced
- 120ml/4floz beef stock

- Bring a pan of water to boil and add in the spaghetti with a pinch of salt. Cook for 12 minutes, or until cooked through and tender.

- Meanwhile, place a frying pan on a medium heat and add in a glug of olive oil. Add in the chopped onion, carrot and a crushed clove of garlic. Cook for 1-2 minutes before adding in the minced beef. Season well with salt and pepper and stir regularly, folding the beef over and moving the mixture around until it is browned and thoroughly cooked through.

- Pour in the beef stock, stir, and allow to simmer for 3-4 minutes. Spoon in 4 tablespoons of tomato puree and mix well. Add a splash of balsamic vinegar and a splash of Worcestershire sauce. Sieve in ½ a tablespoon of cornflower, mix well and allow to simmer for a further 2 minutes.

- Once cooked, drain the spaghetti and serve onto a plate or in a bowl. Spoon the Bolognese sauce on top and serve hot.

Add a generous sprinkling of Parmesan cheese to top this delicious classic off.

Spaghetti and Spicy Meatballs

- 200g/7oz spaghetti
- 125g/4oz minced beef or pork meatballs
- 200g/7oz tinned chopped tomatoes
- 1 red chilli, de-seeded and chopped
- ½ tbsp ground paprika

● Bring a pan of water to boil and add in the spaghetti with a pinch of salt. Cook for 10-12 minutes, or until cooked through and tender.

● Meanwhile, place a frying pan on a medium heat and add in a glug of olive oil. Add in the meatballs and move them around regularly, turning to ensure they cook through thoroughly and evenly. Pour in the tinned tomatoes and crush a clove of garlic into the pan. Add a good pinch of black pepper, as well as the chilli and ground paprika. Allow the mixture to simmer for 3-4 minutes to burn off some of the excess water from the tinned tomatoes. Add a tablespoon of tomato puree to thicken the sauce and mix well.

● Once cooked, drain the spaghetti and serve. Spoon the meatballs and tomato sauce on top. Enjoy whilst still hot.

Add in some onion for more texture, or a large pinch of chilli powder to give a slightly bigger burst of flavour.

Cheesy Vegetable Tricolour Fusilli

SERVES 2

- 150g/5oz mixed root vegetables, cubed
- 200g/7oz tricolour fusilli
- 100g/3½oz passata
- 50g/2oz Parmesan, grated
- A handful of rocket

- Pre-heat the oven to 350F/180C/Gas 4.

- Place the mixed root vegetables in a roasting dish, brush with oil and season generously with salt and pepper. Add in a minced clove of garlic, combining with the mixed vegetables. Cook for 20-25 minutes until tender. If preferred, cover with foil or place a lid on top and cook for 30 minutes for a softer vegetable. Once cooked, remove from the oven and place to one side.

- Meanwhile bring a pan of water to boil. Add in the fusilli and cook for 10-12 minutes, or until cooked through and tender. In a frying pan add a drizzle of olive oil and the roasted vegetables. Pour over the passata. If you prefer lots of sauce with your pasta, add a little more passata.

- Warm the sauce through and add in the grated Parmesan, allowing it to melt. Roughly chop the rocket and stir in as well. Once cooked, drain the pasta and spoon the pasta onto a plate or bowl. Spoon over the tomato sauce to serve.

Try a green chilli for an extra kick to get your taste buds tingling.

Spaghetti alla Carbonara

SERVES 2

- 200g/7oz spaghetti
- 125g/4oz pancetta
- 2 eggs
- 40ml/1½floz single cream
- 50g/2oz Parmesan, grated

- Bring a pan of water to boil and add in the spaghetti with a pinch of salt. Cook for 10 minutes, or until cooked through and tender.

- Meanwhile, place a frying pan on a medium heat and add in a glug of olive oil. Throw in the pancetta and cook through thoroughly. Once cooked, remove from the heat and place to one side.

- While the spaghetti continues to cook, beat together the eggs and the single cream in a small bowl to prepare the carbonara sauce. Season well with salt and pepper.

- Once cooked, drain the spaghetti and return to the pan. Add in the cooked pancetta and stir it through. Then, pour in the egg and cream mixture, along with the grated Parmesan. Return to the heat and stir well so the sauce is warmed through and the cheese melted. Make sure you stir continuously to ensure the sauce does not burn or stick; reduce the heat slightly if necessary.

- Once warmed through, serve straight from the pan and sprinkle over any remaining grated Parmesan.

Serve with some freshly made chunky garlic ciabatta.

Tomato and White Wine Tagliatelle

SERVES 2

- 200g/7oz tagliatelle
- 1 small onion, finely chopped
- 50ml/2oz dry white wine
- 200g/7oz tinned chopped tomatoes with herbs
- A large handful of finely chopped fresh basil

● Bring a pan of water to boil and add in the tagliatelle with a pinch of salt. Cook for 10-12 minutes, or until cooked through and tender.

● Meanwhile, place a frying pan on a medium heat and add in a good drizzle of olive oil. Add in the chopped onion and sauté for 2-3 minutes. Mince a small clove of garlic, add to the pan and cook for a further 30-60 seconds. Pour the white wine into the pan and allow it to simmer for 1-2 minutes, or a little longer if possible. Pour in the chopped tomatoes, along with a tablespoon of tomato puree. Sprinkle in the chopped basil and stir well. Leave to simmer, reducing the heat slightly, for 4-5 minutes so that it reduces and thus thickens.

● Once cooked, drain the tagliatelle and return to the pan. Spoon in the tomato sauce and mix well with the tagliatelle. Serve straight from the pan and enjoy.

A hearty topping of Parmesan cheese can finish this pasta dish off wonderfully.

Creamy Pesto and Parmesan Tagliatelle

SERVES 2

- 200g/7oz tagliatelle
- 100g/3½oz green pesto
- ½ tbsp crème fraiche
- 40g/1½oz Parmesan, grated
- A splash of freshly squeezed lemon juice

- Bring a pan of water to boil and add in the tagliatelle with a pinch of salt. Cook for 10-12 minutes, or until cooked through and tender.

- Once cooked, drain the tagliatelle and return to the pan. Spoon in the green pesto and mix well with the tagliatelle to evenly cover the pasta. Add a pinch of black pepper and spoon in the crème fraiche. Mix well to blend everything and then return to the heat, reducing it slightly. Continuing to stir the pasta and sauce, add in the Parmesan and splash of lemon juice. Mix well and keep stirring until most of the Parmesan has melted. Serve straight from the pan.

A good splash of dry white wine in this sauce could be an excellent addition.

Linguine alla Marinara

- 1 litre/1½ pints mussels
- 200g/7oz linguine
- ½ onion, finely chopped
- 350g/12oz tinned chopped tomatoes
- 1 tbsp freshly chopped parsley

- Place the mussels in a bowl with cold water so that it rises an inch or two above the mussels. If any mussels float to the top or open, discard them.

- Bring a pan of water to boil and add in the linguine. Cook for 10 minutes, or until tender and cooked through. Meanwhile, place all of the remaining mussels in a pan with 75-100ml of water, depending on how many mussels you have left. Cover the pan, bring to the boil and cook for 5-7 minutes, or until all of the mussels have opened. Give the pan a good shake every few minutes.

- In a frying pan, warm a good splash of olive oil through and add in two cloves of minced garlic that along with the onion and tomatoes. Season well with salt and pepper and sprinkle in the parsley. Stir well and allow the mixture to simmer for 1-2 minutes before adding in the cooked mussels. Once all of the mussels have opened, drain any excess water and add them to the tomato sauce in the pan. If some mussels have still not opened after 8 minutes, discard them.

- Once cooked, drain the linguine and return to the pan. Spoon in the mussels and tomato sauce mixture from the pan and stir well to combine. Serve straight from the pan and enjoy.

Paprika Infused Butternut and Broccoli Conchiglie

- ½ butternut squash, peeled and cubed
- 100g/3½oz tender stem broccoli
- 200g/7oz conchiglie pasta
- 75ml/3fl oz vegetable stock
- 1 tsp ground paprika

- Bring 2 saucepan of water to boil. Place the chopped butternut squash in one pan and boil for 7-8 minutes. Add in the broccoli and cook for a further 12 minutes. At the same time as adding the broccoli, add the conchiglie to the other pan of boiling water. Once cooked through, drain the butternut squash and broccoli and return to the pan. Crush a clove of garlic and add it to the butternut squash along with the vegetable stock and paprika. Season well and use a hand blender or food processor to blend until smooth.

- Once cooked, drain the pasta and return to the pan. Pour the sauce from the food processor, or other pan if using a hand blender, over the conchiglie and warm through. Serve straight from the pan.

Top with a sprinkling of Parmesan; pour the pasta into a baking dish and crisp up under the grill for a quick pasta bake style finish.

Chilli Prawn Linguine

SERVES 2

- 200g/7oz linguine pasta
- 75g/3oz fresh, cooked prawns
- 1 small red chilli, de-seeded and chopped
- 200g/7oz tinned chopped tomatoes
- 1 tsp chilli flakes

- Bring a pan of water to boil and add in the linguine.

- Sprinkle in a pinch of salt and cook for 10-12 minutes, stirring occasionally.

- While the pasta cooks, warm a dash of olive in a saucepan on a medium heat.

- Add in a small clove of freshly minced garlic, the red chilli and prawns and cook for 1 minute, stirring regularly. Pour in the chopped tomatoes and chilli flakes and let the mixture simmer for 5-7 minutes on a medium heat.

- Once the prawn and pasta are cooked, drain the linguine and then return it to the pan. Pour over the prawn and chilli sauce and stir well. Remove from the pan and serve whilst hot.

Linguine originated in the Liguria region of Italy. Traditionally linguine is served with seafood or pesto, while spaghetti usually accompanies meat dishes.

Pepper Pasta Salad

SERVES 2

- 200g/7oz conchiglie pasta
- 1 red pepper, de-seeded and finely sliced
- Handful of fresh basil leaves, torn
- ½ tbsp freshly squeezed lemon juice
- 1 tbsp of Parmesan cheese

- Bring a pan of water to boil.

- Add in the conchiglie pasta along with a pinch of salt. Cook the pasta for 10-12 minutes or until thoroughly cooked through. Once cooked, drain and place the pasta into a bowl.

- Add in the chopped red pepper and torn basil leaves and toss well. Add in a splash of olive oil and the lemon juice and toss well again.

- Serve with the Parmesan cheese and enjoy warm or chill and eat cooled later.

Basil is the royal Italian herb. Known as 'basilico' basil is the key herb used time and time again in Italian cooking.

Classic Pepperoni Pasta

- 200g/7oz penne pasta
- 200g/7oz tinned chopped tomatoes with herbs and chilli
- 75g/3oz pepperoni, finely sliced
- 1 tsp ground paprika
- A large pinch of fresh parsley, finely chopped

● Bring a pan of water to boil. Add in the penne pasta with a good pinch of salt and cook for 10-12 minutes.

● Once cooked, drain the pasta and return it to the pan.

● Crush a small clove of garlic and add into the pasta with a pinch of black pepper. Pour in the chopped tomatoes and stir well. Return the pasta and sauce to a low heat to warm through.

● Add the pepperoni slices into the pan, either whole or torn if you prefer, along with the paprika and mix well.

● Once warmed through, serve immediately and top with the freshly chopped parsley.

Use a spicier pepperoni to add a kick and a sprinkling of Parmesan for a truly Italian finish.

nom
nom
ITALY
pizza

Wonderfully Easy Homemade Pizza Dough

- 225g/8oz strong white flour
- 1½ tsp dried active yeast
- 1 tsp sugar
- 100ml/3½floz warm water
- 50ml/2fl oz warm milk

● Add the flour, yeast sugar and a large pinch of salt into a bowl and toss well together. Pour in a tablespoon of olive oil and mix well.

● Gradually pour in the warm water and milk, adding a little to the mixture, stirring it in, and then repeating the process until a dough-like texture is formed. Use your hands to mix and eventually knead.

● Dust a clean, dry work surface with some flour and knead the dough for 5 minutes to create a smooth mixture with an elastic-like texture.

● Move the dough to a clean, dry bowl or dish and cover with a damp tea towel. Leave the dough for 1-2 hours to 'prove'. During this time the dough will rise and should double in size.

● Next, repeat the kneading process and place back in the bowl and cover with a damp tea towel to repeat the rising process also. Divide the dough into two and roll each out, again, onto a clean, dry surface lightly dusted with flour, until an even circular pizza shape is created.

● The dough is now ready to top with your preferred ingredients and then cook in a pre-heated oven for 10-12 minutes.

The Absolutely Classic Margherita Pizza

MAKES 1
PIZZA

- 1 homemade pizza base (see page 76) or large ready-made pizza base
- 3 tbsp passata
- A large handful of cherry tomatoes, sliced
- 75g/3oz mozzarella, sliced
- Fresh basil leaves to garnish

- Pre-heat the oven to 350F/180C/Gas4.

- Place the pizza base on a flat surface that has been dusted lightly with flour to prevent it from sticking.

- Spoon the passata onto the pizza and spread across the base, leaving a border of roughly 1cm around the edge.

- Arrange the sliced tomatoes over the pizza, scattering fairly evenly, and then repeat this method with the sliced mozzarella.

- Place in the oven for 12-15 minutes, unless otherwise instructed for the pre-made pizza base, or until the cheese has melted and the pizza is beginning to crisp.

- Remove from the oven and scatter over the basil leaves to serve.

This simple Italian classic makes an excellent base for a wide range of variations of toppings.

Three Cheese Pizza

- 1 homemade pizza base (see page 76) or large ready-made pizza base
- 3 tbsp passata
- 50g/2oz fontina cheese, grated
- 50g/2oz mozzarella, sliced
- 50g/2oz Parmesan cheese, grated

- Pre-heat the oven to 350F/180C/Gas4.

- Place the pizza base on a flat surface that has been dusted lightly with flour to prevent it from sticking.

- Spoon the passata onto the pizza and spread across the base. Leaving a border of roughly 1cm around the edge allows a slight crust to crisp.

- Using each of the cheeses, sprinkle, cover and arrange them as you wish.

- Place in the oven for 12-15 minutes, or until all of the cheese has melted and the pizza is beginning to crisp.

- Remove from the oven and slice to serve.

A sprinkling of dried mixed herbs can add a little flavour to this cheesy wonder.

Ultimate Garlic Pizza Bread

MAKES 1 PIZZA

- 1 homemade pizza base (see page 76) or large ready-made pizza base
- 2 tbsp butter
- A large pinch of dried mixed herbs
- 5 garlic cloves, crushed
- Fresh parsley to garnish

- Pre-heat the oven to 350F/180C/Gas4.

- Place the pizza dough on a flat surface that has been dusted lightly with flour to prevent it from sticking. Roll the dough out to create a pizza base, ensuring a fairly even thickness all around and creating an oval or oblong shaped base.

- Place in the oven and cook for 5-7 minutes to allow the dough to begin to rise.

- Combine the crushed garlic into the butter with a fork.

- Remove the base from the oven and spread the garlic butter across the base, using more butter if required, to ensure it is generously covered. Sprinkle across some dried mixed herbs and parsley and return to the oven for a further 5-7 minutes, or until the base is thoroughly cooked and the top is beginning to crisp, but not burned.

- Remove from the oven and cut into strips to serve.

Top with slices of Parmesan for a cheesy variation.

Mixed Pepper Pizza

- 1 homemade pizza base (see page 76) or large ready-made pizza base
- 3 tbsp passata
- 2 sweet peppers, de-seeded and cut into strips
- 1 red onion, finely diced
- 50g/2oz mozzarella, sliced

- Pre-heat the oven to 350F/180C/Gas4.

- Place the pizza base on a flat surface that has been dusted lightly with flour to prevent it from sticking.

- Spoon the passata onto the pizza and spread across the base, leaving a border of roughly 1cm around the edge to allow a crust to crisp.

- Scatter the red onion across the base. Arrange the pepper strips and mozzarella slices across the pizza and season with black pepper.

- Place in the oven for 12-15 minutes, unless otherwise instructed for the pre-made pizza base. The pepper strips should be softening and beginning to crisp.

- Remove from the oven and slice to serve.

For a fiery kick, finely chop a red chilli and mix with the red onion before scattering over the pizza.

Deliciously Italian Pepperoni

- 1 homemade pizza base (see page 76) or large ready-made pizza base
- 3 tbsp passata
- 50g/2oz mozzarella, sliced
- 125g/4oz sliced mixed sized pepperoni
- 25g/1oz cheddar, grated

- Pre-heat the oven to 350F/180C/Gas4.

- Place the pizza base on a flat surface that has been dusted lightly with flour to prevent it from sticking. Spoon the passata onto the base and spread across the base leaving a border of roughly 1cm around the edge.

- Arrange the sliced mozzarella across the pizza, breaking the pieces up to cover different areas if needed, then arrange the pepperoni slices as well. The pepperoni can overlap the mozzarella, although an even coverage of both is ideal.

- Sprinkle across where any gaps are the cheddar, adding more if necessary, season with black pepper and place in the oven. Cook for 12-15 minutes, unless otherwise instructed for the pre-made pizza base. Remove from the oven and slice to serve.

The portions are just a guideline; add more cheese and pepperoni as desired. A spicier sausage can provide a hotter variation of this absolute classic.

Chilli and Roasted Pepper Pizza

MAKES 1 PIZZA

- 1 homemade pizza base (see page 76) or large ready-made pizza base
- 3 tbsp passata
- 2 red chillies, de-seeded and sliced
- 4 roasted peppers, sliced (from a jar)
- 75g/3oz mozzarella, torn

● Pre-heat the oven to 350F/180C/Gas4.

● Place the pizza base on a flat surface that has been dusted lightly with flour to prevent it from sticking.

● Crush a clove of garlic into the chilli passata and spoon onto the pizza, spreading it across the base. Leave a border of roughly 1cm around the edge. Arrange the chillies and peppers over the base, along with the torn mozzarella.

● Place in the oven for 12-15 minutes, unless otherwise instructed for the pre-made pizza base, or until the cheese has melted and the pizza is beginning to crisp. Remove from the oven and slice to serve.

Not for the faint hearted, this pizza is best served with a cooling dip to soothe off your taste buds.

Pizza alla Napoletana

- 1 homemade pizza base (see page 76) or large ready-made pizza base
- 3 tbsp passata
- 75g/3oz mozzarella, sliced
- 25g/1oz tinned anchovies
- Fresh basil leaves to garnish

- Pre-heat the oven to 350F/180C/Gas4.

- Place the pizza base on a flat surface that has been dusted lightly with flour to prevent it from sticking.

- Spoon the passata onto the pizza and spread across the base, leaving a border of roughly 1cm around the edge. Depending on the size of your pizza base, you may need an extra spoonful of passata to ensure a fair covering.

- Arrange the sliced mozzarella across the pizza. Again, you may wish to add a little more depending on your preference and pizza base size, as the mozzarella is key for a napoletana.

- Scatter over the anchovies and garnish with torn, fresh basil leaves.

- Place in the oven for 12-15 minutes, unless otherwise instructed for the pre-made pizza base, or until the cheese has melted and the pizza is beginning to crisp. Remove from the oven and slice to serve.

A simple yet extremely flavourful Italian classic; you can easily adjust the topping quantities to suit your preference.

Classic yet Simple Pizza Marinara

- 1 homemade pizza base (see page 76) or large ready-made pizza base
- 3 tbsp passata
- A large handful of cherry tomatoes, sliced
- 75g/3oz mozzarella, sliced
- ½ tbsp freshly chopped oregano

- Pre-heat the oven to 350F/180C/Gas4.

- Place the pizza base on a flat surface that has been dusted lightly with flour to prevent it from sticking.

- Spoon the passata onto the pizza and spread across the base, leaving a border of roughly 1cm around the edge.

- Arrange the chopped cherry tomatoes over the pizza, scattering fairly evenly.

- Crush 2 cloves of garlic and scatter over the pizza before arranging the sliced mozzarella in a similar manner spreading fairly evenly.

- Sprinkle over the chopped oregano, then cook in the oven for 12-15 minutes, unless otherwise instructed for the pre-made pizza base, or until the cheese has melted and the pizza is beginning to crisp. Remove from the oven and slice to serve.

Garlic and oregano really stand out on this pizza, injecting a new flavours absent from the traditional margherita or napolenta.

Broccoli and Red Onion Pizza

MAKES 1 PIZZA

- 1 homemade pizza base (see page 76) or large ready-made pizza base
- 3 tbsp passata with mixed herbs
- 75g/3oz mozzarella, torn
- ½ head broccoli florets, sliced into flat cross sections
- 1 red onion, sliced

- Pre-heat the oven to 350F/180C/Gas4.

- Place the pizza base on a flat surface that has been dusted lightly with flour to prevent it from sticking. Spoon the passata onto the pizza and spread across the base, leaving a border of roughly 1cm around the edge.

- Depending on the size of your pizza base, you may need an extra spoonful of passata.

- Arrange the torn mozzarella over the pizza and top with the broccoli florets and red onion. You may wish to save a little of the mozzarella to place slightly over some of the broccoli or red onion.

- Place in the oven for 12-15 minutes. Remove from the oven and slice to serve.

If you prefer your broccoli tender, pre-boil the broccoli before adding to the pizza so it is partly cooked.

Red Pepper, Feta and Spinach Pizza

MAKES 1
PIZZA

- 1 homemade pizza base (see page 76) or large ready-made pizza base
- 3 tbsp passata
- 1 red pepper, sliced
- ½ small red onion, sliced
- 75g/3oz feta, crumbed

● Pre-heat the oven to 350F/180C/Gas4.

● Place the pizza base on a flat surface that has been dusted lightly with flour to prevent it from sticking.

● Next, spoon the passata onto the pizza and spread evenly across the base ,leaving a border of roughly 1cm around the edge.

● Add the sliced red pepper and red onion ensuring an even coverage of the pizza, then crumble feta over the pizza in a similar manner.

● Place the pizza in the oven for 12-15 minutes, unless otherwise instructed for the pre-made pizza base, or until the cheese has melted and the pizza is beginning to crisp.

● Remove from the oven and drizzle over a splash of balsamic vinegar to serve.

Garnish with spinach leaves for added colour and texture.

Green Pesto Pizza

- 1 homemade pizza base (see page 76) or large ready-made pizza base
- 4 tbsp green basil pesto
- A large handful of cherry tomatoes, sliced
- 1 small red onion, chopped
- 75g/3oz feta, crumbled

- Pre-heat the oven to 350F/180C/Gas4. Place the pizza base on a flat surface that has been dusted lightly with flour to prevent it from sticking.

- Spoon the pesto onto the pizza and spread across the base, leaving a border of roughly 1cm around the edge. Add a little more pesto if required, depending on the size of your pizza.

- Evenly scatter the chopped tomatoes and red onion over the pizza and then repeat with the crumbed feta.

- Place in the oven for 12-15 minutes, unless otherwise instructed for the pre-made pizza base, or until the cheese has melted and the pizza is beginning to crisp.

- Remove from the oven and slice to serve.

This tasty pizza is full of flavour. Add chicken if you like for an extra protein hit.

Vegan Hummus Pizza

MAKES 1
PIZZA

- 1 homemade pizza base (see page 76) or large ready-made pizza base
- ½ red bell pepper, de-seeded and sliced
- 4 mushrooms, sliced
- 3 tbsp red pepper hummus
- 75g / 3oz vegan mozzarella cheese, sliced

- Pre-heat the oven to 350F/180C/Gas4.

- Add a splash of olive oil to a frying pan, and over medium heat, sauté the peppers and mushrooms until soft. Set the vegetables aside to use as toppings shortly.

- Place the pizza base on a flat surface that has been dusted lightly with flour to prevent it from sticking.

- Spoon the red pepper hummus onto the pizza and evenly spread it across the base ,leaving a border of roughly 1cm around the edge.

- Next, arrange the sautéed vegetables over the pizza, scattering fairly evenly, and then repeat this method with the shredded vegan mozzarella.

- Place in the oven for 12-15 minutes, unless otherwise instructed for the pre-made pizza base, or until the cheese has melted and the pizza is beginning to crisp.

- Remove from the oven and drizzle with a little olive oil to serve.

This flexible vegan recipe is an excellent base for a wide range of toppings.

Balsamic Goat's Cheese and Fig Pizza

MAKES 1
PIZZA

- 1 homemade pizza base (see page 76) or large ready-made pizza base
- 3 tbsp passata with garlic
- ½ red onion, chopped
- 3 fresh figs, sliced
- 75g/3oz goat's cheese sliced

- Pre-heat the oven to 350F/180C/Gas4.

- Place the pizza base on a flat surface that has been dusted lightly with flour to prevent it from sticking. Next, spoon the passata onto the pizza and spread across the base leaving a border of roughly 1cm around the edge of the pizza.

- Depending on the size of the pizza base, you may require an extra tablespoon or two of passata.

- To cut the figs make sure you remove the stems first, and then slice in half and in half again.

- Add the chopped red onions, sliced figs and the goats cheese to the pizza making sure to arrange the toppings evenly.

- Place in the oven for 12-15 minutes, unless otherwise instructed for the pre-made pizza base, or until the cheese has melted and the pizza is beginning to crisp.

- Remove from the oven and drizzle over a little balsamic vinegar to serve.

This interesting take on pizza beautifully pairs sweet balsamic with fresh figs.

Spicy BBQ Chicken Pizza

MAKES 1
PIZZA

- 1 homemade pizza base (see page 76) or large ready-made pizza base
- 3 tbsp spicy barbeque sauce
- 1 small skinless chicken breast, cooked and chopped
- ½ small red onion, chopped
- 75g/3oz mozzarella, sliced

- Pre-heat the oven to 350F/180C/Gas4.

- Place the pizza base on a flat surface that has been dusted lightly with flour to prevent it from sticking.

- Spoon the barbeque sauce onto the pizza and spread across the base, leaving a border of roughly 1cm around the edge

- Next, arrange the chicken and red onion over the pizza, scattering fairly evenly, and then repeat this method with the sliced mozzarella.

- Place in the oven for 12-15 minutes, unless otherwise instructed for the pre-made pizza base, or until the cheese has melted and the pizza is beginning to crisp.

- Remove from the oven and slice to serve. Drizzle over a little olive oil if needed.

The spicy BBQ gives this pizza a delicious kick. Enjoy with chopped bacon for another variation.

Chilli Chicken and Ricotta Pizza

- 1 homemade pizza base (see page 76) or large ready-made pizza base
- 3 tbsp passata with chillies
- 1 skinless chicken breast, cooked and chopped
- ½ orange pepper, de-seeded and thinly sliced
- 75g/3oz Ricotta cheese

- Pre-heat the oven to 350F/180C/Gas4.

- Place the pizza base on a flat surface that has been dusted lightly with flour to prevent it from sticking.

- Spoon the chilli passata onto the pizza and spread evenly across the base, leaving a border of roughly 1cm around the edge.

- Then, arrange the sliced pepper and chicken over the pizza, scattering fairly evenly, and then repeat this method with the feta.

- Place in the oven for 12-15 minutes, unless otherwise instructed for the pre-made pizza base, or until the cheese has melted and the pizza is beginning to crisp.

- Remove from the oven and slice to serve.

Italian ricotta is typically made from the whey of sheep, cow, goat, or Italian water buffalo milk.

The Bolognese Inspired Pizza

MAKES 1 PIZZA

- 1 homemade pizza base (see page 76) or large ready-made pizza base
- 75g/3oz lean minced beef
- Handful of mushrooms, chopped
- 3 tbsp passata with garlic
- 75g/3oz mozzarella, sliced

- Pre-heat the oven to 350F/180C/Gas4.

- Heat a good splash of olive oil in a frying pan over a medium heat and add in the minced beef. Season with salt and pepper and crush in a small clove of garlic. Cook for 8-10 minutes, stirring regularly, or until browned.

- Meanwhile, place the pizza base on a flat surface that has been dusted lightly with flour to prevent it from sticking. Spoon the passata onto the pizza and spread evenly across the base leaving a border of roughly 1cm around the edge of the pizza.

- Once cooked drain the mincemeat and place evenly across the pizza. Next, arrange the mushrooms over the pizza, scattering fairly evenly, and then repeat this method with the sliced mozzarella cheese.

- Place in the oven for 12-15 minutes, unless otherwise instructed for the pre-made pizza base, or until the cheese has melted and the pizza is beginning to crisp. Remove from the oven and slice to serve.

The earliest documented recipe for a meat-based sauce (ragù) comes from late 18th century Imola, near Bologna.

CONVERSION CHART: DRY INGREDIENTS

Metric	Imperial
7g	¼ oz
15g	½ oz
20g	¾ oz
25g	1 oz
40g	1½oz
50g	2oz
60g	2½oz
75g	3oz
100g	3½oz
125g	4oz
140g	4½oz
150g	5oz
165g	5½oz
175g	6oz
200g	7oz
225g	8oz
250g	9oz
275g	10oz
300g	11oz
350g	12oz
375g	13oz
400g	14oz

Metric	Imperial
425g	15oz
450g	1lb
500g	1lb 2oz
550g	1¼lb
600g	1lb 5oz
650g	1lb 7oz
675g	1½lb
700g	1lb 9oz
750g	1lb 11oz
800g	1¾lb
900g	2lb
1kg	2¼lb
1.1kg	2½lb
1.25kg	2¾lb
1.35kg	3lb
1.5kg	3lb 6oz
1.8kg	4lb
2kg	4½lb
2.25kg	5lb
2.5kg	5½lb
2.75kg	6lb

CONVERSION CHART: LIQUID MEASURES

Metric	Imperial	US
25ml	1fl oz	
60ml	2fl oz	¼ cup
75ml	2½ fl oz	
100ml	3½fl oz	
120ml	4fl oz	½ cup
150ml	5fl oz	
175ml	6fl oz	
200ml	7fl oz	
250ml	8½ fl oz	1 cup
300ml	10½ fl oz	
360ml	12½ fl oz	
400ml	14fl oz	
450ml	15½ fl oz	
600ml	1 pint	
750ml	1¼ pint	3 cups
1 litre	1½ pints	4 cups

YOU MAY ALSO ENJOY...

**Eat & Feast Well. Waste Less, Save Money & Time
Recipes for Family of 4 at £1 per head**

Minotaur Press, a Top Cow Productions Company, Presents...

WILDFIRE ™

Created by
Matt Hawkins & Linda Sejic

published by
Top Cow Productions, Inc.
Los Angeles

Minotaur Press, a Top Cow Productions Company, Presents...

WILDFIRE™

Matt Hawkins
Co-Creator & Writer

Linda Sejic
Co-Creator & Artist

Troy Peteri
Letterer

Cover art by
Linda Sejic

Original editions edited by
Betsy Gonia

Production by Tricia Ramos

To find the comic shop
nearest you, call:
1-888-COMICBOOK

COMIC SHOP LOCATOR SERVICE
888-266-4226

Want more info? Check out:
www.topcow.com
for news & exclusive Top Cow merchandise!

TOP COW
PRODUCTIONS, INC.

TOP COW PRODUCTIONS, INC.
Marc Silvestri - CEO
Matt Hawkins - President & COO
Betsy Gonia - Managing Editor
Elena Salcedo - Operations Manager
Ryan Cady - Editorial Assistant
Vincent Valentine - Production Assistant

CARTHAY CIRCLE PUBLISHING

CARTHAY CIRCLE PUBLISHING
Brian K. Altounian - CEO
Jacob Morris - COO

IMAGE COMICS, INC.
Robert Kirkman – Chief Operating Officer
Erik Larsen – Chief Financial Officer
Todd McFarlane – President
Marc Silvestri – Chief Executive Officer
Jim Valentino – Vice-President

Eric Stephenson – Publisher
Ron Richards – Director of Business Development
Jennifer de Guzman – Director of Trade Book Sales
Kat Salazar – Director of PR & Marketing
Corey Murphy – Director of Retail Sales
Jeremy Sullivan – Director of Digital Sales
Emilio Bautista – Sales Assistant
Branwyn Bigglestone – Senior Accounts Manager
Emily Miller – Accounts Manager
Jessica Ambriz – Administrative Assistant
Tyler Shainline – Events Coordinator
David Brothers – Content Manager
Jonathan Chan – Production Manager
Drew Gill – Art Director
Meredith Wallace – Print Manager
Monica Garcia – Senior Production Artist
Addison Duke – Production Artist
Tricia Ramos – Production Assistant
IMAGECOMICS.COM

image

Wildfire Volume 1. Trade Paperback.
DECEMBER 2014. FIRST PRINTING. ISBN: 978-163215-024-0, $14.99 U.S.D.

Dan Miller **Violet Silva** **Mick O'Connell**

(Plant Biologists)

Ashley Miller **Beth Silva**

(Sister to Dan Miller) (GMO Researcher)

**Michelle
Crawford** **Sheila
Todd**

(KCLA News Reporters)

Chapter One

PRO

"Recall that world food output will need to at least double and possibly triple over the next several decades. Even if production could be increased that much using conventional technology, which is doubtful, the required amounts of pesticide and fertilizer and other polluting chemicals would be immense.
If properly developed, disseminated, and used, genetically modified crops might well be the best hope the planet has got."

Dr. Jonathan Rauch

CON

"The genetic modification of food is intrinsically dangerous. It involves making irreversible changes in a random manner to a complex level of life about which little is known.

It is inevitable that this hit-and-miss approach will lead to disasters. It must disrupt the natural intelligence of the plant or animal to which it is applied, and lead to health-damaging side-effects."

Dr. Geoffrey Clements

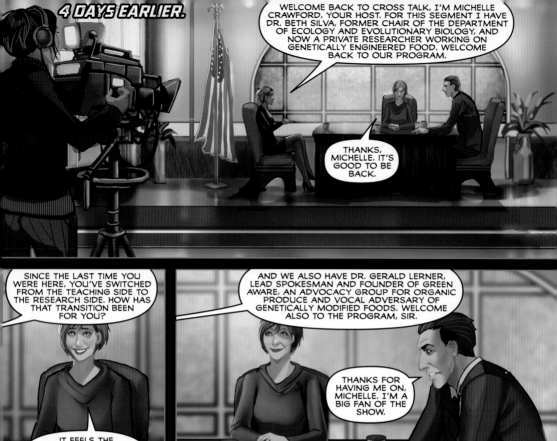

4 DAYS EARLIER.

WELCOME BACK TO CROSS TALK, I'M MICHELLE CRAWFORD, YOUR HOST. FOR THIS SEGMENT I HAVE DR. BETH SILVA, FORMER CHAIR OF THE DEPARTMENT OF ECOLOGY AND EVOLUTIONARY BIOLOGY, AND NOW A PRIVATE RESEARCHER WORKING ON GENETICALLY ENGINEERED FOOD. WELCOME BACK TO OUR PROGRAM.

THANKS, MICHELLE. IT'S GOOD TO BE BACK.

SINCE THE LAST TIME YOU WERE HERE, YOU'VE SWITCHED FROM THE TEACHING SIDE TO THE RESEARCH SIDE. HOW HAS THAT TRANSITION BEEN FOR YOU?

IT FEELS THE SAME. I'M STILL ON CAMPUS WORKING WITH PROMISING YOUNG MINDS TRYING TO MAKE THE WORLD A BETTER PLACE.

AND WE ALSO HAVE DR. GERALD LERNER, LEAD SPOKESMAN AND FOUNDER OF GREEN AWARE, AN ADVOCACY GROUP FOR ORGANIC PRODUCE AND VOCAL ADVERSARY OF GENETICALLY MODIFIED FOODS. WELCOME ALSO TO THE PROGRAM, SIR.

THANKS FOR HAVING ME ON, MICHELLE. I'M A BIG FAN OF THE SHOW.

THERE'S BEEN A LOT OF DISCUSSION AND CONTROVERSY ABOUT *GMO*, GENETICALLY MODIFIED ORGANISMS, IN THIS CASE SPECIFICALLY GENETICALLY ENGINEERED FOOD. *GE FOOD* AS THEY CALL IT.

WE'VE HEARD TERMS LIKE *FRANKENFOOD* TOSSED AROUND. DR. LERNER, LET'S START WITH YOU. TELL US ABOUT GREEN AWARE AND WHY YOU'RE SO OPPOSED TO THESE *GE FOODS*.

I STARTED *GREEN AWARE* WHEN I REALIZED THAT COMPANIES WERE GENETICALLY ALTERING SEEDS, FOOD, AND ANIMALS WITHOUT ANY OVERSIGHT FROM THE GOVERNMENT.

CREATING POTENTIALLY DEADLY ORGANISMS, PURPOSEFULLY OR ACCIDENTALLY, COULD ALTER OUR ECOSYSTEM FOREVER.

ONE COMPANY I WON'T NAME, BECAUSE THEY LITIGATE LIKE MAD, HAS CORNERED THIS MARKET AND PATENTED THOUSANDS OF SLIGHT GENETIC VARIATIONS. THEY NOW HAVE MONOPOLY CONTROL THAT OUR GOVERNMENT ALLOWS.

Dr. Gerald Lerner
Founder of Green Aware

WHY? I DON'T KNOW. I CAN'T GET A SINGLE MEMBER OF CONGRESS TO LOOK ME IN THE EYE AND TELL ME WHY THEY ALLOW THIS.

SO I STARTED MY OWN FOUNDATION, WITH MY OWN MONEY, AND HAVE STARTED RAISING AWARENESS.

OUR CITIZENS SHOULD NOT BE USED AS UNWITTING GUINEA PIGS.

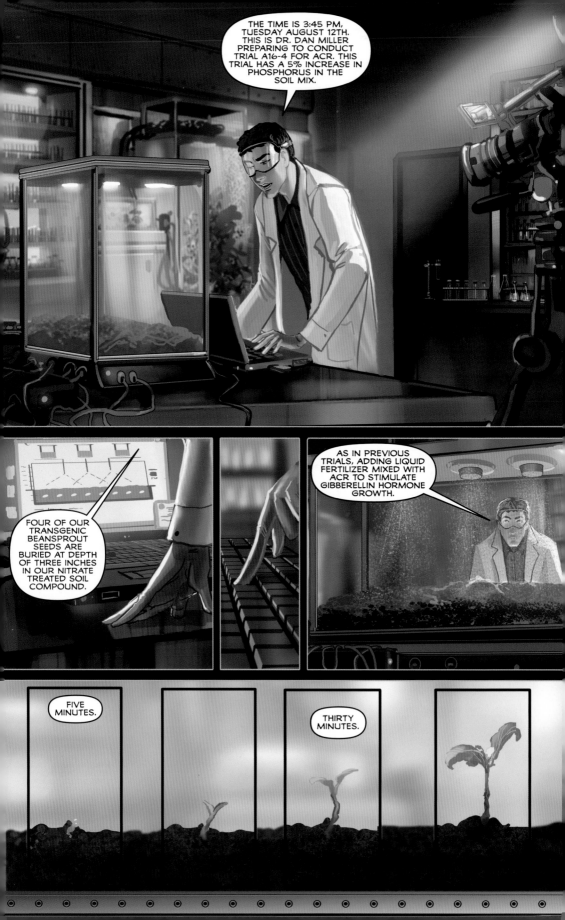

YEAH, I'M SO OVER BIEBER, HE'S DISGUSTING NOW.

YOUR SISTER IS NO LONGER A BELIEBER?

SHUT UP AND IGNORE HER, PLEASE. IT'S HARD ENOUGH TO FOCUS WITH HER BABBLING ENDLESSLY ON THE PHONE.

I DON'T UNDERSTAND WHY THE STABILIZATION AGENTS DON'T WORK.

YEAH, WITHOUT THAT IT JUST ENDS IN DESICCATION.

THEORETICALLY IT SHOULD WORK.

YEAH, HE'S HERE. HE'S WORKING, OF COURSE. OKAY I'LL TELL HIM. BYE.

WOULD REVERSE OSMOSIS HELP ELIMINATE ANY UNKNOWN CONTAMINANTS?

WE TRIED THAT IN THE A-12 TRIALS, BUT WE STILL NEED AN ANSWER FOR CONTAMINANTS. FARM FIELDS AREN'T STERILE ENVIRONMENTS.

THAT WAS VIOLET.

SHE SAID SHE WANTED TO COME OVER TONIGHT AND YOU SAID NO. WHAT'S YOUR PROBLEM?

I MEAN, I DON'T GET WHY SHE'S EVEN INTO YOU, SHE'S HOT. YOU'RE NEVER GOING TO DO BETTER THAN THAT.

I DON'T WANT HER AROUND YOU, ASH, SHE'S A BAD INFLUENCE. YOU KNOW IT. I KNOW IT. END OF STORY.

I'VE TRIED TO LOOK AFTER YOU, YA KNOW, EVER SINCE MOM DIED. THIS ISN'T EASY ON ME EITHER, LIVING WITH A 15-YEAR-OLD SISTER.

LOOK, I KNOW I SCREWED UP. I REALIZE WE'RE NOT READY TO GO PUBLIC WITH THIS YET, BUT THE DAMAGE IS DONE. I CAN'T UN-RING THAT BELL, AND *BIOGENESIS* WANTS US TO HAVE A VERY PUBLIC DEMONSTRATION TO SHOW PEOPLE WHAT WE'RE DOING.

THEY'VE GOTTEN A LOT OF BAD PRESS IN RECENT YEARS--

SOME OF IT DESERVED.

YES, SOME OF IT MUCH DESERVED. THEY ARE, HOWEVER, OUR FUNDING.

WITHOUT THEM WE SHUT DOWN, AND THE UNIVERSITY WON'T CONTINUE THE PROGRAM WITHOUT OUTSIDE MONEY. WE'RE ALL LOOKING FOR JOBS.

HOW MANY OF YOU KNOW SOMEONE WHO'S BEEN LOOKING FOR A JOB FOR OVER A YEAR? I DO.

DO YOU REALLY WANT TO BE LOOKING FOR JOBS IN THIS ECONOMY?

NO? OKAY THEN. WE'RE GOING WITH WHAT WE HAVE. I'VE BOOKED THE AUDITORIUM FOR 3:30 TOMORROW AFTERNOON, JUST IN TIME FOR THE EVENING NEWS ON BOTH COASTS.

EVERYONE WILL PREP, BUT IT WILL JUST BE DAN AND ME ON THE PODIUM.

YOU'LL BE CONDUCTING THE EXPERIMENT AND WE'LL BOTH BE NARRATING THE PROCESS. KEEP IT SIMPLE AND EXPLAIN WHAT YOU'RE DOING AS YOU CONDUCT, AND I'LL ADD ANALYSIS.

AND WHAT DO WE DO WHEN THEY SEE HOW QUICKLY THE BEAN SPROUTS WILT?

I'VE THOUGHT ABOUT THAT. WE CAN'T USE BEAN SPROUTS ANYWAY--TOO MUCH NEGATIVITY ASSOCIATED WITH THE WHOLE JACK AND THE BEANSTALK STUFF.

WE NEED SOMETHING UNIVERSALLY KNOWN, HARMLESS, AND INNOCUOUS. SOMETHING THAT WITH A QUICK DEMISE WON'T MATTER BECAUSE ITS END PROCESS ISN'T SEEN AS A FAILED YIELD.

TARAXACUM OFFICINALE. IT'S SEXUALLY COMPATIBLE WITH THE VARIETIES WE'VE BEEN TESTING. IT'S ALSO ONE OF THE 200 PLANTS WE DEVELOPED TRANSGENIC SEEDS FOR, SO WE *CAN* USE IT.

YOU WANT US TO SHOWCASE WITH A PLANT WE'VE NOT TESTED ON YET?

IT'S A ONE-TIME CONTAINED TEST IN ONE OF THE HYDROPONIC CHAMBERS WE CAN WHEEL UP ON STAGE. A QUICK DOG AND PONY SHOW TO KEEP US ALL EMPLOYED AND WORKING.

IT'S NOT OPTIMAL, BUT LET'S STAY FOCUSED ON THE PRIZE HERE. I BELIEVE IN WHAT WE'RE DOING, SO DO ALL OF YOU. IF WE NEED TO CUT A COUPLE CORNERS TO KEEP THE FUNDING GOING SO WE CAN ACHIEVE THAT, I SAY IT'S WORTH IT.

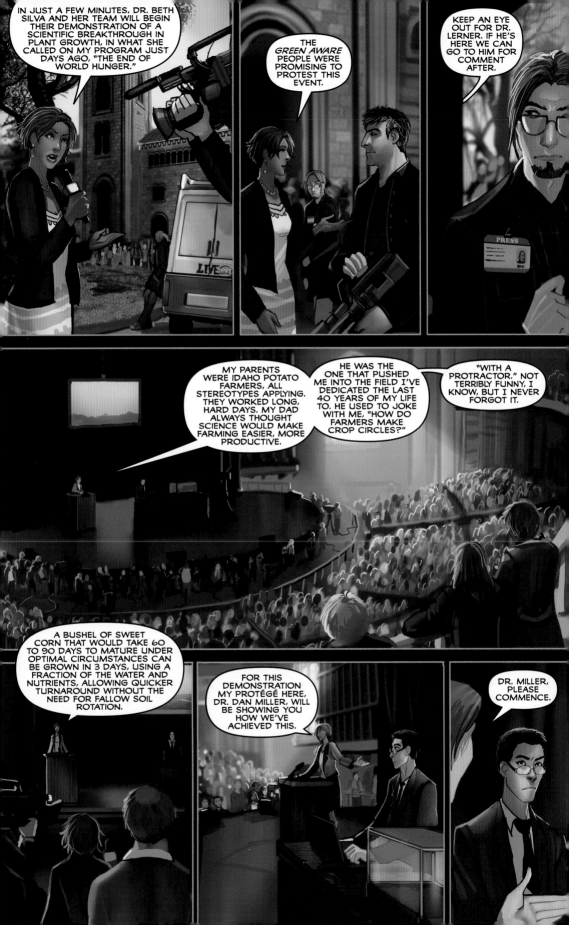

THANK YOU, DR. SILVA. WHAT WE WILL BE DEMONSTRATING IS HOW THE PROCESS WORKS. STEP ONE IS USING OUR TRANSGENIC SEEDS THAT WE DEVELOPED IN OUR OXNARD FACILITY.

SINCE WE DIDN'T ASSUME YOU'D WANT TO SIT THERE AND WATCH THE PLANT GROW FOR A FEW DAYS, WE'RE USING A FAST GROWING PLANT TO SHOWCASE. SOMETHING EVERYONE KNOWS-- A DANDELION.

THERE ARE TWELVE OF THESE SEEDS ALREADY PLANTED IN THE SOIL.

KEEP IN MIND, WE'RE USING IDEAL CIRCUMSTANCES HERE AND SPECIALLY TREATED SOIL, WHICH WILL BE FAR MORE DIFFICULT TO DUPLICATE IN THE FIELD--

--BUT VERY DOABLE. WE'VE SUCCESSFULLY EXPERIMENTED WITH OVER 100 SEED VARIETIES IN ONE OF OUR OUTDOOR GREENHOUSES.

ACR, THE CATALYZING AGENT TO INITIATE THE PROCESS, IS MIXED WITH LIQUID FERTILIZER. ONCE POURED ON THE TREATED SOIL, THE PROCESS SHOULD BEGIN QUICKLY.

IT WILL TAKE A FEW MINUTES. THANKS FOR YOUR PATIENCE.

Chapter Two

1. The terms "genetically modified organism" (GMO) and "genetically modified foods" (GM foods) refer to plants or animals whose genes have been changed in the laboratory by scientists. All living organisms have genes written in their DNA. They are the chemical instructions for building and maintaining life. By modifying the genes, scientists can alter the characteristics of an organism. In agriculture, genetic engineering allows simple genetic traits to be transferred to crop plants from wild relatives, other distantly related plants, or virtually any other organism. Manipulating the genetics of foods is not new.

- Michael Murray, N.D. and Joseph Pizzorno, N.D.,
The Encyclopedia of Healing Foods

2. We have entered an era of genetically modified foods, which are just that -- genetically mutated foods that are not necessarily better for you. The health implications not only to humans but also to the environment is a hotly contested debate; the introduction of genetically altered food could have serious consequences, such as allergic reactions and increased resistance to certain antibiotics. Two of the prime targets for genetic engineering -- soy and corn -- are America's cash crops.

- Brenda Watson and Leonard Smith,
The Detox Strategy: Vibrant Health in 5 Easy Steps

8:30 AM

UM... WHAT'S GOING ON HERE?

AH, MR. MILLER. WE'VE BEEN WAITING FOR YOU.

THAT'S *DR.* MILLER.

FOR NOW. I'M AGENT MARK CHEN WITH THE FBI.

DR. SILVA IS BEING INTERVIEWED. THEY WANT TO SPEAK WITH YOU NEXT.

WELL, I WANT TO HELP. I BROUGHT IN SOME FIELD SPECIMENS WE CAN TEST FOR THE *ACR* COMPOUND.

THAT WON'T BE NECESSARY, BELIEVE ME. WE HAVE A LOT OF SAMPLES ALREADY AND PEOPLE COLLECTING MORE. WE'RE AWARE OF IT AFFECTING OTHER DANDELION VARIANTS.

COME WITH ME, DAN. THIS IS AN UNUSUAL CASE WITH A LOT OF AGENCIES INVOLVED. RIGHT NOW WE'RE JUST TRYING TO GET AHEAD OF IT.

THE *DHS, FEMA, FDA,* AND *CDC* HAVE PUT TOGETHER A JOINT TASK FORCE IN UNDER THREE HOURS AND HAVE ALREADY ISSUED A QUARANTINE ZONE, ALTHOUGH IT'S NOT PUBLIC YET.

SOME POWERFUL PEOPLE SEEM PANICKED AND AREN'T SAYING WHY...AND THAT SCARES ME.

I NEED YOU TO EXPLAIN TO ME HOW *ACR* WORKS.

THE POINT OF ORIGIN WAS THE PRESS CONFERENCE YESTERDAY. AN EARLY MAP OF ITS SPREAD LINES UP WITH WIND PATTERNS.

VIDEO SHOWS THAT AFTER THE GLASS CASE WAS BROKEN, THE ACTIVIST HAD DANDELION SEEDS ON HIS JACKET.

SO WE KNOW HOW IT GOT OUT. THE QUESTION IS HOW DO WE STOP IT FROM SPREADING FURTHER?

ANY WEED KILLER WILL WORK; THESE SEEDS WEREN'T DESIGNED TO BE RESISTANT TO PESTICIDE. I'M SURE BIOGENESIS WILL HELP WITH THAT.

BIOGENESIS HAS ALREADY WALLED THEMSELVES BEHIND LAWYERS AND IS DISTANCING ITSELF FROM YOU.

WHAT?!

ACCORDING TO THEIR CHIEF COUNSEL YOU ARE, "AN INDEPENDENT LAB OPERATING UNDER UNIVERSITY RESEARCH OVERSIGHT."

DEAN HORMEL, WE CAN'T LET THE UNIVERSITY TAKE THE BLAME FOR THIS.

EXACTLY, BETH. WE'VE KNOWN EACH OTHER FOR A LONG TIME, BUT YOU'VE REALLY SCREWED UP HERE. THE TRUSTEES WANT YOU OUT.

PLEASE, DON'T DO THIS. MY TEAM AND I CAN FIX THIS.

I MISS YOU, MOM. WISH YOU WERE HERE TO TELL ME IT'S GOING TO BE OKAY.

I'M ABOUT TO LOSE MY CAREER AND ASHLEY HATES ME. SHE NEEDS YOU. I DON'T KNOW HOW TO TALK TO HER.

Can you pick up Ashley from school? No clue how long this will take.

Violet

Oh so when you need me I'm not a bad influence? J/K I'll get her. hope you're ok <3

We'll be @ ur place. Check this link, it's getting hairy out there.

the News down under

LOS ANGELES OVERRUN BY WEEDS QUARANTINE BEING CONSIDERED?

OTHER NEWS

MAN SURVIVES AN AVALANCHE
read more

SCIENCE STUDY: CATS THAT SHOW AFFECTION ARE HAPPY
read more

TOP TEN MOST DANGEROUS CUTLERY PIECES YOU POSSESS IN YOUR HOME
read more

FEAR IS STARTING TO GRIP LOS ANGELES AS FEMA HAS ISSUED A TEMPORARY QUARANTINE FOR PARTS OF THE WEST SIDE, AND ALL TRAFFIC IN OR OUT OF THE QUARANTINE AREA HAS BEEN STOPPED.

CLICK

THE CITY AND VARIOUS OTHER STATE AND FEDERAL GOVERNMENT AGENCIES HAVE BEEN VISIBLY ACTIVE ALL OVER, BUT HAVE BEEN SEEMINGLY UNABLE TO DO MUCH TO SLOW THE RAPIDLY GROWING WEEDS.

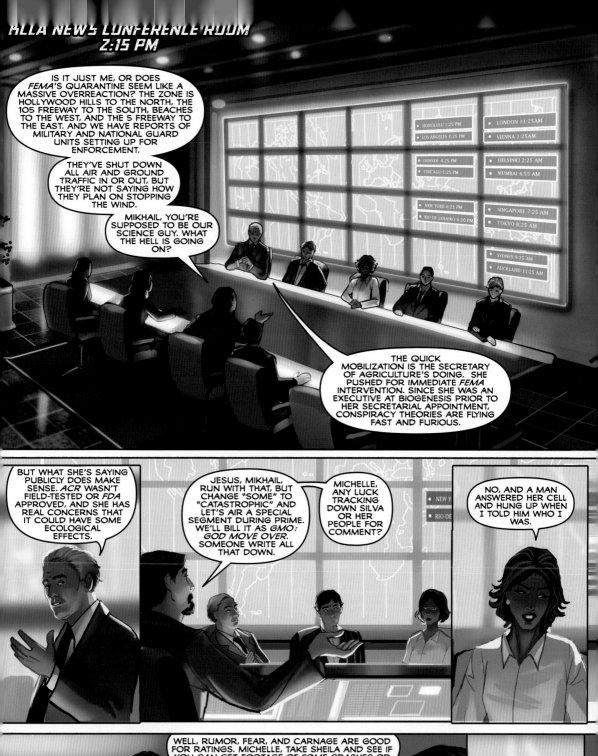

IS IT JUST ME, OR DOES *FEMA*'S QUARANTINE SEEM LIKE A MASSIVE OVERREACTION? THE ZONE IS HOLLYWOOD HILLS TO THE NORTH, THE 105 FREEWAY TO THE SOUTH, BEACHES TO THE WEST, AND THE 5 FREEWAY TO THE EAST. AND WE HAVE REPORTS OF MILITARY AND NATIONAL GUARD UNITS SETTING UP FOR ENFORCEMENT.

THEY'VE SHUT DOWN ALL AIR AND GROUND TRAFFIC IN OR OUT, BUT THEY'RE NOT SAYING HOW THEY PLAN ON STOPPING THE WIND.

MIKHAIL, YOU'RE SUPPOSED TO BE OUR SCIENCE GUY. WHAT THE HELL IS GOING ON?

- HONOLULU 1:25 PM
- LOS ANGELES 3:25 PM
- LONDON 11:25AM
- VIENNA 1:25AM
- DENVER 4:25 PM
- CHICAGO 5:25 PM
- HELSINKI 2:25 AM
- MUMBAI 4:55 AM
- NEW YORK 6:25 PM
- RIO DE JANEIRO 8:30 PM
- SINGAPORE 7:25 AM
- TOKYO 8:25 AM
- SYDNEY 9:25 AM
- AUCKLAND 11:25 AM

THE QUICK MOBILIZATION IS THE SECRETARY OF AGRICULTURE'S DOING. SHE PUSHED FOR IMMEDIATE *FEMA* INTERVENTION. SINCE SHE WAS AN EXECUTIVE AT BIOGENESIS PRIOR TO HER SECRETARIAL APPOINTMENT, CONSPIRACY THEORIES ARE FLYING FAST AND FURIOUS.

BUT WHAT SHE'S SAYING PUBLICLY DOES MAKE SENSE. *ACR* WASN'T FIELD-TESTED OR *FDA* APPROVED, AND SHE HAS REAL CONCERNS THAT IT COULD HAVE SOME ECOLOGICAL EFFECTS.

JESUS, MIKHAIL, RUN WITH THAT, BUT CHANGE "SOME" TO "CATASTROPHIC" AND LET'S AIR A SPECIAL SEGMENT DURING PRIME. WE'LL BILL IT AS *GMO: GOD MOVE OVER.* SOMEONE WRITE ALL THAT DOWN.

MICHELLE, ANY LUCK TRACKING DOWN SILVA OR HER PEOPLE FOR COMMENT?

NO, AND A MAN ANSWERED HER CELL AND HUNG UP WHEN I TOLD HIM WHO I WAS.

- NEW Y
- RIO DE

WELL, RUMOR, FEAR, AND CARNAGE ARE GOOD FOR RATINGS. MICHELLE, TAKE SHEILA AND SEE IF YOU CAN GET FOOTAGE OF SOME CRASHES OR SOMETHING WORTH WATCHING.

YOU'VE BEEN LISTENING TO ALL THINGS CONSIDERED ON KCRW. NEXT UP, WE HAVE DR. GERALD LERNER FROM *GREEN AWARE* JOINING THE PROGRAM.

TICK TOCK

DR. LERNER, WELCOME TO ALL THINGS CONSIDERED HERE ON NPR. WHAT ARE YOUR THOUGHTS ON THE EVENTS UNFOLDING IN LOS ANGELES?

AND I'M OFF THE GRID.

NO SIGNAL

COMPLETELY.

IT'S THE REALIZATION OF MY GREATEST FEAR. WE'VE RELEASED SOMETHING INTO THE ENVIRONMENT THAT IS CHANGING THE VERY BIOSPHERE ITSELF.

UH...HI. I'VE BEEN WAITING FOR AGENT CHEN FOR ALMOST FIVE HOURS NOW. I'M HUNGRY, HAD TO PEE IN A STARBUCKS CUP, AND NOW YOU'VE OBVIOUSLY BLOCKED MY PHONE AND INTERNET ACCESS. I'D LIKE TO SPEAK TO ONE OF THE UNIVERSITY'S LEGAL STAFF, PLEASE.

UNDER *FEMA* QUARANTINE YOU'RE NOT ENTITLED TO SPEAK TO COUNSEL.

IS THAT TRUE?

LOOK IT UP ON THE INTERNET.

BUT YOU BLOCKED... NEVER MIND.

THE GOVERNMENT HAS BEEN LESS THAN FORTHCOMING WITH INFORMATION, WHICH IS NEEDLESSLY CAUSING FEAR AND PANIC AMONG THE PEOPLE IN THE QUARANTINE AREA.

BEFORE REAL DISASTER STRIKES.

HEY, ASH.

HEY, VIOLET.

FIGURES YOU'D BE PICKING ME UP.

WHY DO YOU SAY THAT?

EVERYONE'S TALKING ABOUT THE QUARANTINE AND MY MAD SCIENTIST BROTHER.

HE'S NOT VICTOR FRANKENSTEIN. YOU SHOULDN'T TALK ABOUT HIM LIKE THAT.

YOU JUST DEFEND HIM BECAUSE YOU WANT HIS BOD...AND I DO NOT KNOW WHY. LOOK AT THE MESS HE MADE.

TRAFFIC IS BAD. WE SHOULD HEAD TO YOUR PLACE AND WAIT FOR DAN.

HARD TO BELIEVE THERE'S SO MUCH TRAFFIC SINCE PEOPLE ARE SUPPOSED TO GO HOME AND STAY THERE.

PEOPLE DON'T WANT TO BE TOLD WHAT TO DO.

LET'S SEE WHAT THE RADIO HAS TO SAY.

...SWEEPING SOUTH QUICKLY.

WE CAN'T WAIT ANY LONGER, THAT FIRE IS SECONDS AWAY. LIFTING OFF.

WHAT?

ROOF EXIT

Chapter Three

"An ecosystem, you can always intervene and change something in it, but there's no way of knowing what all the downstream effects will be or how it might affect the environment. We have such a miserably poor understanding of how the organism develops from its DNA that I would be surprised if we don't get one rude shock after another."

Professor Richard Lewontin, Professor of Genetics, Harvard University

"But we realize that with any new and powerful technology with unknown, and to some degree unknowable - by definition - effects, then there necessarily will be an appropriate level at least, and maybe even more than that, of public debate and public interest."

Bob Shapiro, Chief Executive of Monsanto

THIS IS MICHELLE CRAWFORD FOR KCLA NEWS. LOS ANGELES IS ON FIRE. FROM DOWNTOWN TO MIDTOWN TO THE BEACH CITIES THE WHOLE CITY IS ENGULFED IN FLAMES WITH VERY LITTLE CONTAINMENT REPORTED AS OF YET.

EMERGENCY SERVICES ARE OVERWHELMED AS EVACUATIONS CONTINUE TO CONTAINMENT AREAS. CASUALTIES ARE EXPECTED TO BE IN THE HUNDREDS OF THOUSANDS AS WHAT WAS ONCE THE CITY OF ANGELS IS NOW A CITY OF ASH.

OKAY, MY TURN.

WHAT? THAT WAS LIVE, DEAR. WE DON'T NEED YOU TO DO ANOTHER ONE. YOU'RE HERE TO OBSERVE AND LEARN.

THAT'S NOT WHAT BOB SAID. TELL HER, J.J.

UH, SHEILA, YEAH, BOB SAID FOR HER TO SHOOT AS WELL. THEY'LL USE HERS ON THE WEB SITE.

THIS IS SHEILA TODD FOR KCLA NEWS. LOS ANGELES IS ON FIRE. FROM DOWNTOWN TO MIDTOWN TO THE BEACH CITIES -- THE WHOLE CITY IS ENGULFED IN FLAMES WITH VERY LITTLE CONTAINMENT REPORTED AS OF YET.

EMERGENCY SERVICES ARE OVERWHELMED AS EVACUATIONS CONTINUE TO CONTAINMENT AREAS. CASUALTIES ARE EXPECTED TO BE IN THE HUNDREDS OF THOUSANDS AS WHAT WAS ONCE THE CITY OF ANGELS IS NOW A CITY OF ASH.

MY EXACT WORDS.

MY HAIR LOOK OKAY IN THAT?

PEOPLE ARE DYING AND YOU'RE WORRIED ABOUT YOUR *HAIR*?

YOU LOOK GREAT.

HEY, NOT ALL OF US CAN GET AWAY WITH THE MOTHERLY LOOK.

EXCUSE ME?

DR. MARCUS, WELCOME TO LOS ANGELES. THE CITY IS A MESS. CASUALTIES COULD BE IN THE MILLIONS. ELECTRICITY, CABLE, CELLULAR, WATER...ALL DOWN...WE'VE ESTIMATED IT WILL TAKE WEEKS TO GET BASIC SERVICES BACK UP AND RUNNING.

WE'VE BEEN BROADCASTING AND DROPPING PAMPHLETS TELLING PEOPLE TO EVACUATE BUT A LOT OF PEOPLE ARE INSIDE THEIR HOMES WHERE WE TOLD THEM TO GO BEFORE THE FIRE BROKE OUT.

THAT, FOLLOWED BY THE COMMUNICATIONS BLACK OUT, MEANS A WHOLE LOT OF PEOPLE DON'T KNOW TO EVACUATE AND ARE STILL IN THE ZONE.

THANKS FOR THE UPDATE, AGENT CHEN. SINCE CAL TECH HAS ITS OWN GENERATOR WE SHOULD BE FINE HERE UNLESS WE NEED TO MOVE AGAIN.

THE PRESIDENT HAS GIVEN ME FULL SITUATIONAL AUTHORITY WITH MY *FEMA* TEAM. COLONEL DAVIS HAS BEEN ASSIGNED AS LIAISON FOR THE MILITARY.

HAS THERE BEEN ANY WORD ON DR. SILVA?

SHE'S BEEN CONFIRMED DEAD. HER NUMBER TWO, DR. DAN MILLER, IS HERE IF YOU WANT TO TALK TO HIM.

YES, HAVE DR. MILLER SENT UP TO GIVE US A COMPLETE BRIEFING. I'VE READ THE REPORTS BUT I'D LIKE TO HEAR IT FROM HIS MOUTH.

SOUNDS GOOD, SAY AN HOUR?

PERFECT.

OKAY, SHEILA, YOUR TURN.

AS IF L.A. DIDN'T HAVE ENOUGH TO DEAL WITH, AN EARTHQUAKE WITH A MAGNITUDE OF 4.7 STRUCK JUST EAST OF WESTWOOD ABOUT AN HOUR AGO.

SEVERAL SMALLER AFTERSHOCKS HAVE ALREADY BEEN REPORTED AND WE'VE BEEN TOLD MORE ARE EXPECTED.

THESE QUAKES HAVE NOT EASED THE FIRE SITUATION AND RESPONDERS ARE REPORTING NEW OUTBREAKS AND A SETBACK TO 40% CONTAINMENT DESPITE INCREASED USE OF PLANES AND DRONES TO DROP FIRE RETARDANT CHEMICALS.

THE CITY CONTINUES TO TAKE A BEATING AND EVACUATIONS HAVE BEEN STEPPED UP FROM ALL BORDERS OF THE QUARANTINE ZONE.

FOR THOSE OF YOU WITH ACCESS TO MEDIA INSIDE THE ZONE PLEASE COMMUNICATE THE EVACUATION ORDER TO YOUR NEIGHBORS AND ANYONE YOU SEE AS MANY HAVE NOT RECEIVED THIS NEWS YET.

THAT'S ALL FOR NOW, I'M SHEILA TODD REPORTING FOR KCLA NEWS.

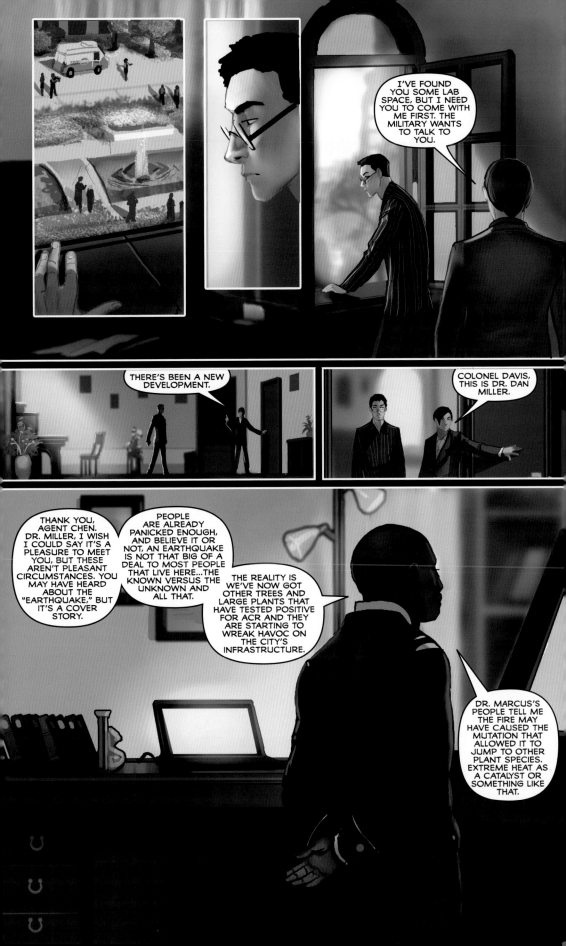

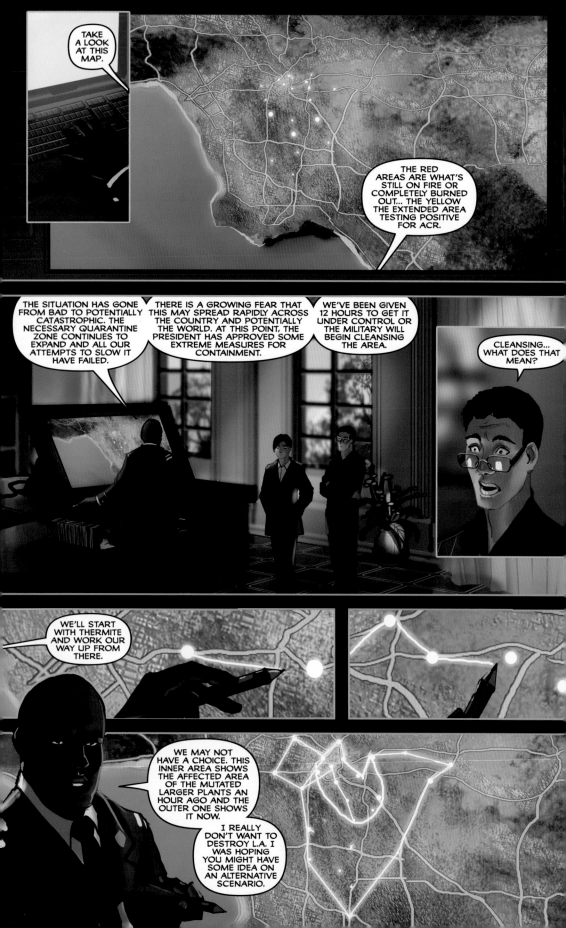

MISS CRAWFORD.

DR. MILLER? ARE YOU OKAY?

LOOK, I DON'T HAVE MUCH TIME TO EXPLAIN BUT THESE EARTHQUAKES AREN'T QUAKES AT ALL.

THEN WHAT'S GOING ON?

TREES AND BIGGER PLANTS ARE GROWING, THERE'S NO FIRE THERE. HELP ME FIND MY SISTER AND GET TO AN EVAC POINT AND I'LL GIVE YOU THE WHOLE STORY.

MY APARTMENT IS WEST OF SEPULVEDA, DESTROYING THE CITY'S INFRASTRUCTURE. THE GOVERNMENT IS GOING TO BOMB L.A. OUT OF EXISTENCE TO STOP IT.

JJ, LET'S GO.

HOW DO WE GET PAST THE CHECKPOINTS?

I'LL WORRY ABOUT THAT WHEN WE GET THERE.

Chapter Four

"There is no credible evidence that GMO foods are safe to eat."

- David Schubert, Salk Institute of Biological Studies

"Every major international science body in the world has reviewed multiple independent studies, in some cases numbering in the hundreds, in coming to the consensus conclusion that GMO crops are as safe or safer than conventional or organic foods. But until now, the magnitude of the research on crop biotechnology has never been cataloged. In response to what they believed was an information gap, a team of Italian scientists summarized 1783 studies about the safety and environmental impacts of GMO foods—a staggering number."

- Jon Entine, executive director of the Genetic Literacy Project, & a senior fellow at the Center for Health & Risk Communication and STATS(Statistical Assessment Service) at George Mason University.

I REALIZE YOU MIGHT BE LOOKING FOR SOMETHING TO GIVE YOUR LIFE MEANING IN YOUR TWILIGHT YEARS, BUT I DIDN'T SIGN ON FOR THIS TO PUT MY LIFE IN DANGER.

CAN WE KNOCK THIS CRAP OFF? BOTH OF YOU. WE'RE INSIDE THE QUARANTINE ZONE, PROBABLY THE ONLY NEWS TEAM HERE. I RESPECT YOUR JOURNALISTIC INTEGRITY, BUT WE CAN'T REPORT THE TRUTH IF WE'RE DEAD.

LET'S GET TO DAN'S PLACE, GRAB HIS SISTER, SHOOT SOME B-ROLL, AND GET THE HELL OUT OF HERE AS FAST AS WE CAN.

NO, WE NEED TO GO BACK NOW!

THERE IS NO HEADING BACK.

YOU CAN GET OUT AND WALK IF YOU WANT.

COLONEL DAVIS, I HAVE UPDATES FOR YOU, SIR.

WE'VE CONFIRMED FAILURE FOR ALL SEVEN FIELD-TESTS, INCLUDING THE WEED KILLER DEVELOPED BY DR. MARCUS'S TEAM. THE PLANT GROWTH IS STILL OUTPACING CONTAINMENT EFFORTS, AND THE ZONE CONTINUES TO EXPAND.

THE LARGER TREE GROWTH HAS KNOCKED DOWN MOST OF THE SKYSCRAPERS ON THE WEST SIDE. CENTURY CITY IS GONE COMPLETELY...

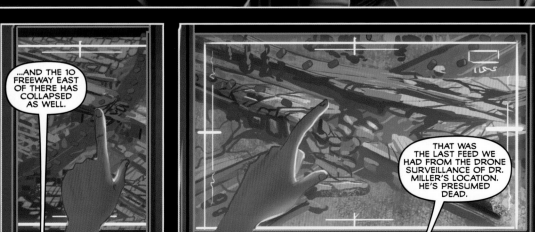

...AND THE 10 FREEWAY EAST OF THERE HAS COLLAPSED AS WELL.

THAT WAS THE LAST FEED WE HAD FROM THE DRONE SURVEILLANCE OF DR. MILLER'S LOCATION. HE'S PRESUMED DEAD.

FIRE CREWS ARE ALSO REPORTING CONTAINMENT AT LESS THAN THIRTY PERCENT WITH NEW FIRES--

THAT WILL BE ALL, THANK YOU.

SITCOM, THIS IS COLONEL DAVIS. I WANT THOSE BIRDS IN THE AIR NOW.

ACKNOWLEDGED, SIR.

FOXTROT, PACKAGE IS CLEARED FOR LAUNCH. YOU WILL PROCEED TO TARGET ZONE AND CIRCLE, AND AWAIT FURTHER ORDER.

IT WON'T BE LONG BEFORE THIS THING SPREADS UP HERE. BETTER WE WASTE SOME FUEL THAN GET CAUGHT FLAT-FOOTED.

WE'VE STILL GOT A FEW HOURS BEFORE THE CUTOFF, GET DR. MARCUS BACK ON THE LINE.

HOW MUCH LONGER DO WE HAVE TO WAIT?

CONTAMINATION PROTOCOLS ARE FOR EVERYONE'S SAFETY, AND WE HAVE DIFFERENT LEVELS OF CONTAINMENT. WE'RE WAITING FOR YOUR TEST RESULTS, SHOULDN'T BE MUCH LONGER.

ARE THERE PHONES ABOARD WE CAN USE? THE CELL PHONES AREN'T WORKING.

YES, THERE ARE COMM TOWERS ABOARD.

VROOOOM

ASHLEY!

DAN!

OH ASH, I'M SO GLAD YOU'RE OKAY. I WAS SO WORRIED ABOUT YOU.

WE WALKED ALL THE WAY FROM HOME, AND I WOULD HAVE DIED IF VIOLET HADN'T SAVED ME. THE GROUND OPENED UP AND TRIED TO SWALLOW ME, BUT SHE PULLED ME OUT. I WAS SO SCARED.

I'M SO GLAD YOU'RE SAFE. I LOVE YOU, ASH.

VIOLET.

HEY, DAN.

THANK YOU. I'M SORRY I EVER DOUBTED YOU.

WAIT...

WHERE'S MY MOM? I THOUGHT YOU TWO WOULD BE TOGETHER?

VIOLET... I'M SO SORRY... SHE WAS KILLED IN THE FIRE AT THE UNIVERSITY.

WHAT?

MISS, WE'LL NEED YOU TO RETEST NOW THAT HE MAY HAVE CONTAMINATED YOU BY TOUCH.

ALL FOUR OF YOU HEAD UP THIS RAMP. SHOULDN'T TAKE TOO LONG.

YOUR COOPERATION WILL BE APPRECIATED.

YES, OF COURSE, I'LL DO WHATEVER YOU WANT. MY NAME IS DR. DAN MILLER. IF YOU COULD GET WORD TO COLONEL DAVIS, HE'LL WANT TO KNOW MY LOCATION.

THOSE PLANES ARE FLYING LOW OVER THE CITY. I DON'T KNOW IF THAT'S A GOOD OR BAD THING.

HAVE YOU SPOKEN FURTHER WITH COLONEL DAVIS?

YEAH, HE MADE NO PROMISES, BUT SAID THAT MICK HAD ALREADY SHOWN A POSITIVE RESULT IN THE LAB.

THAT'S FIRE RETARDANT THEY'RE DROPPING. IF THEY'RE TRYING TO STOP THE FIRE AGAIN, I THINK THAT'S A GOOD SIGN. THEY'VE GOT PEOPLE ON THE WAY TO PICK US UP.

"DR. DAN MILLER, IT'S GREAT TO SEE YOU AGAIN, AND THANKS FOR COMING ON THE SHOW. IT'S BEEN THREE MONTHS NOW SINCE LOS ANGELES, AND A LOT OF UNANSWERED QUESTIONS STILL LINGER.

"OVER THREE HUNDRED THOUSAND PEOPLE CONFIRMED DEAD, FIFTY THOUSAND STILL MISSING AND PRESUMED DEAD, MILLIONS HOMELESS, AND TRILLIONS IN PROPERTY DAMAGE. ESTIMATES ARE IT WILL TAKE FIFTEEN YEARS TO REBUILD THE CITY."

THE FALLOUT HAS BEEN INTENSE. THE SECRETARY OF AGRICULTURE RESIGNED. BIOGENESIS'S STOCK DROPPED EIGHTY PERCENT. THE FBI RAIDED GREEN AWARE'S BELLINGHAM FACILITY.

THE SHEER VOLUME OF LAWSUITS AND INDICTMENTS HAS BEEN STAGGERING. ALL HEADLINES BEING HOTLY DEBATED AS PEOPLE WANT SOMEONE TO BLAME FOR ALL THIS WITH FINGERS POINTING EVERYWHERE.

AND YET YOU...CENTRAL TO THE CREATION OF ACR AND AT THE PRESS CONFERENCE WHERE IT WAS RELEASED, AND WITH ME WHEN YOU DEVISED THE STRATEGY TO STOP THE MUTATED ACR FROM SPREADING FURTHER...YOU'VE BEEN INVISIBLE FOR THE PAST THREE MONTHS.

WHERE HAVE YOU BEEN? HOW HAVE YOU AVOIDED PROSECUTION? HOW ARE YOU ABLE TO SPEAK WITH ME TODAY?

HEH, WELL, A PROMISE IS A PROMISE FOR MY BEING HERE ON YOUR SHOW. THANKS AGAIN FOR HELPING ME FIND MY SISTER. AND REGARDING MY TIME OVER THE PAST THREE MONTHS, I'M NOW WORKING FOR THE GOVERNMENT, AND THEY'VE BEEN KEEPING ME BUSY.

SO YOU SOLD YOUR SOUL TO STAY OUT OF JAIL?

HAH, NOTHING LIKE THAT. I'M WORKING WITH THE FDA TO MORE CLOSELY MONITOR THE EFFECTS OF GENETICALLY MODIFIED FOOD ON THE ENVIRONMENT, AND DESIGN TESTS TO CHALLENGE THE CLAIMS MADE BY COMPANIES DEVELOPING THEM.

THAT SOUNDS LIKE A GOOD THING.

Science Class

SCIENCE CLASS

Welcome to the first volume of *Wildfire*! I appreciate you picking up this book, and I hope you like it. If you did and can spread the word like wildfire (heh), nothing calls attention to a book like a friendly recommendation or word of mouth. I'd greatly appreciate it. If you bought this hoping this was an anti-GMO propaganda piece, you're going to be a little disappointed. I do feel it's a balanced look at the possible dangers of GMO proliferation. I'm also not a mouth piece for any GMO company; I've never received any money from anyone in this field. I don't think they'll like this fictional story at all, by the way. It focuses on a real, potential risk of letting untested genetic variants into the environment which leads to a mass disaster. Do you consume GMO food? Yes, you probably do. Unless you ONLY eat food that says CERTIFIED ORGANIC on it or specifically says it doesn't contain GMO, then you probably are. Restaurants and fast food use a lot of it. The other real issue with trying to NOT eat GMO is that organic food is way more expensive.

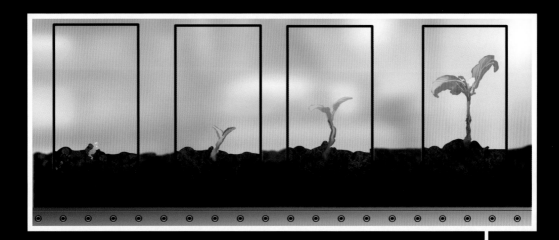

GENETICALLY MODIFIED ORGANISMS (GMO)

I'm sure you've heard this term before but what does it mean?

What is genetic engineering?

> Genetic engineering is the name for certain methods that scientists use to introduce new traits or characteristics to an organism. For example, plants may be genetically engineered to produce characteristics to enhance the growth or nutritional profile of food crops. While these technique are sometimes referred to as "genetic modification," FDA considers "genetic engineering" to be the more precise term. Food and food ingredients from genetically engineered plants were introduced into our food supply in the 1990s.

That definition is from the FDA's website which also has some interesting commentary on how they test these products and how they're "safe." Note also that it says 1990s. Truth is, you've been eating GMO food for decades and you probably didn't even know it. Is it possible that this has contributed to the obesity problem we're facing now? In my personal opinion, the answer to that is both yes and no. The biggest cause of obesity is sugar intake, and food manufacturers have systematically been adding sugar to EVERYTHING over the past few decades because we as consumers like it better. But I'm veering from the main topic. Here's the link for the FDA:

http://www.fda.gov/food/foodscienceresearch/biotechnology/ucm346030.htm

GMO includes animals as well. There are genetically altered fish, chickens, and cows, and, yes, you've probably eaten that already as well.

The prevailing argument is to create more food to thwart growing populations and world hunger. There's a statistic I read that says about every two seconds worldwide a child dies from starvation. That's hard for us in the U.S. to fathom since we're all so fat and well fed for the most part, but take a trip to India (I did) and you'll see some starving people. There are starving people here in the U.S. as well. We just choose not to notice them.
How would they increase food yield?

1) Insect resistant plants —- farmers lose a lot of their crops to insects who eat them. Creating insect resistant GMO plants would either kill the insect if it ate it or make it unpalatable for them. Either way, they stop eating it and the farmer's yield goes way up without having to use more water, more land, and -- the biggest plus -- more pesticides to kill the insects.

2) Herbicide tolerant plants – the idea here is you make plants that are resistant to certain kinds of weed killer. That way you can spray your crops and only kill the weeds. This is one of the more "controversial" pro arguments.

3) Disease resistant plants – Same thing really, but we lose a LOT of crops to various plant diseases like blight, browning, etc. You design plants to resist these.

4) Cold tolerant – Design plants that can grow in colder climates and you vastly increase your farmable land.

5) Drought tolerant – Opposite of the previous point, but same concept that would open up areas of usable land and use less water.

6) Longer shelf life plants – This means designing plants to rot or "go bad" more slowly. This allows additional time for distribution and more time for it to be consumed.

These all sound great and are the utopian ideal of it all. The issue isn't just food growth as we currently grow more food than we need, but getting the food to areas that actually need it. In the U.S. alone, enough food is wasted to currently feed a large percentage of the parts of the world that need it. This comes down to that thing my mom used to say when I was staring at food I didn't want to eat. "There are starving kids in Africa, you should eat that." My response was always, "then send it to them." Ah the wisdom of children! Distribution is a huge problem. Most countries would prefer to grow their own food than have to import it and be susceptible to the whims of the world market economy. Many of the "ideals" of GMO would allow countries to grow more of their food.

CON ARGUMENT FOR GMO ●——————————

The primary argument against GMO is that we're releasing unregulated, un-thoroughly-tested variants into the environment without knowing what the long term effects might be. There's a great concern over the environmental effects and how it might affect us that consume it as well. All good things to discuss! Let's look at some of the arguments:

1) Direct effects on humans who consume – This includes possible tissue/organ damage, compromised immune system, increased fat and enhanced allergic reactions. These are legion and the most immediately concerning. The biggest issue with this is the unknown. The "allergens" thing is interesting. I don't recall many kids with peanut allergies back in the 70's, but there seem to be a lot of them now.

2) Cross pollination – This is a real problem, as non-GMO-plants have seeds, and these GMO seeds tend to float on the wind to far distances. We've found GMO breeds of corn in Mexico, thousands of miles from where they were initially planted. Organic farmers and some countries do not want GMO strains, and having the seeds float into their crops is troublesome to say the least.

3) Insect resistance – Any time you up your game, nature ups it as well. If we create plants that are resistant to certain insects, those insects will also naturally select over time to override said resistance.

4) Weed resistance – Same as the previous point here, but for plants. The logic here is the same as why our overuse of antibiotics is a huge issue as well. It becomes a cycle where you constantly have to evolve these things for this to keep working.

5) Long term environmental effects – This is sort of broad sweeping and covers a lot of detail, but the main concern (and valid) is we really don't know what these things will do over the long haul.

6) Lack of real testing – This is another issue that is hotly debated, but I tend to fall on the activist side of things here. These things need better testing and government oversight. European governments are WAY more concerned about this than we seem to be here in the U.S.

http://healthresearchfunding.org/pros-cons-genetically-modified-foods/
http://www.csa.com/discoveryguides/gmfood/overview.php
http://www.newportnaturalhealth.com/2013/07/gmos-the-pros-cons-of-genetically-modified-food/

IS GMO A NEW THING?

Not really. We've not been doing it previously the way we're doing it now, but farmers have been cross-pollinating breeds and doing genetic enhancement on their own by taking seeds from the stronger plants and replanting those for millennia.

WHAT KINDS OF FOODS ARE GMO?

The big 10 are corn, soy, cottonseed, papaya, rice, canola, potatoes, tomatoes, dairy (milk, cheese, yogurt) and peas.

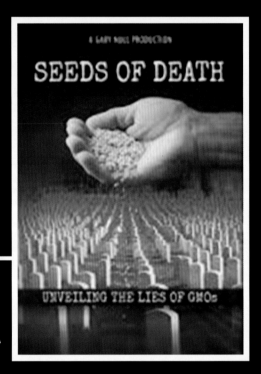

A GARY NULL PRODUCTION

SEEDS OF DEATH

UNVEILING THE LIES OF GMOs

SEEDS OF DEATH ●━━━━━━

This is a free documentary film, very anti-GMO, but informative and entertaining to watch (so much of this shit is so dry).

https://www.youtube.com/watch?v=eUd9rRSLY4A

COMPANIES THAT USE GMO INGREDIENTS

This is not a complete list, but I was looking at pages and pages of listings, and just wrote down the ones whose products I know I've used recently:

Blue Sky, Coca Cola, Hansen, Kraft, Nestle, Procter and Gamble, Libby's, Ocean Spray, Kellogg, Nature Valley, Nabisco, Hershey, Lifesaver, Quaker, Pepperidge Farm, Campbells, Frito Lay, Hostess, Heinz, Crisco, Kashi, Peter Pan, Smuckers, Skippy, Hormel, Progresso, Eggo, Boca, Marie Callender, Morningstar Farms, Stouffers, Betty Crocker, Pillsbury, Aunt Jemima, Duncan Hines, Beech-Nut, Enfamil, Good Start, Similac, Isomil, Yoplait, Land O Lakes, Keebler and Dannon.

If you have thoughts on GMO or this story and want to share them with me, you can hit me up on Facebook or Twitter. I have barely scratched the surface of this and the issues revolving around it. Fortunately, there's more Science Class to discuss this. =)

NOTE – I have started a very self-serving web site called matttalks.com (three t's in the middle there), and am both blogging and posting all Science Classes there with HARD LINKS! You can just go there and click without having to copy the URL.

http://matttalks.com/

Let me start by acknowledging that I am not a plant expert. Not even close. I have no special degrees or education in this field. I was interested and did a lot of research because I was curious. I discovered a lot of fascinating things while doing that, and then made this story up. As promised, I wanted to delve into how they make GMOs and their history a bit.

GMOs ARE NOT NEW

"Scientists and farmers have been genetically modifying food crops since the late 1800's through a process known as hybridization or selective plant breeding. This was the pre-biotechnology method of introducing genetic materials from one individual plant to another."

https://ag.arizona.edu/yavapai/anr/hort/byg/archive/geneticallymodifiedcrops1.html

There is a mistaken assumption that the creation of GMO foods is a modern thing and only possible through genetic engineering. While the past 20 years have really had the most advancement in this field we've ever seen, farmers have basically been doing the same thing for a really long time.

MONSANTO

The leading biotech company was founded in 1901 with the introduction of Sweet and Low.

Here is Monsanto's own history page where you can learn more about them:

http://www.monsanto.com/whoweare/pages/monsanto-history.aspx

And here's one that doesn't like Monsanto much:

http://www.naturalnews.com/037289_monsanto_corporations_ethics.html#

People tend to vilify Monsanto, but there are a lot of scientists that DO work for Monsanto that really want to make the world a better place. There's enough hate for the company online; it's easy to find.

How Crops Are Genetically Modified

Traditional Breeding

Crossing plants and selecting offspring

Almost All Crops

Mutagenesis

Exposing seeds to chemicals or radiation

RNA Interference

Switching off selected genes with RNA

Transgenics

Inserting selected genes using recombinant DNA methods

Number of Genes Affected

10K - >300K	? No way to assess	1 - 2	1 - 4

Desired gene(s) inserted with other genetic material. No safety testing requirements.	Random changes in genome, usually unpredictable. No safety testing requirements.	Targeted gene(s) switched off or 'silenced'. Safety testing required.	Desired gene(s) inserted only at known locations. Safety testing required.

GENETIC LITERACY PROJECT
WHERE SCIENCE TRUMPS IDEOLOGY

Sources: Biotechnology Provides New Tools for Plant Breeding, University of California Davis Publication 8043; Plant Breeding: Induced Mutation Technology for Crop Improvement, F.J. Novak, H. Brunner, International Atomic Energy Agency, 1992; Atomic Gardens: Public Perceptions and Public Policy, B. Dick, M. Jones, Life Sciences Foundation Magazine; RNAi for Crop Improvement, International Service for the Acquisition of Agri-Biotech Applications Pocket K No. 34. **Infographic by XiaoZhi Lim**

MODERN BEGINNING OF GMOs

The modern use of GMOs and transgenic plans started in the 1980s when scientists discovered they could transfer pieces of DNA between organisms. The first transgenic plant was a tobacco plant in 1983, engineered to be resistant to antibiotics, and cotton followed in 1990. The real boom of GMOs started when Monsanto introduced herbicide-immune soy beans known as "round-up ready". They would sell the seeds and the herbicide to the same farmers as part of a package. Shortly after this it was discovered that vitamins and nutrients could be added to plants.

"Why do scientists say that genetic engineering of crops is just the latest chapter in 10,000 years of high-tech agriculture? Or that genetic engineering is just a more precise way to breed plants compared to conventional breeding? Plants swap genes even without the help of human beings when they reproduce sexually, and our ancestors guided the process to develop crops suitable for agriculture. This GLP infographic presents four main ways in which crops have been genetically modified by humans: traditional breeding, mutagenesis, RNA interference and transgenics."

http://www.geneticliteracyproject.org/2014/04/22/glp-infographic-how-crops-are-modified-are-gmos-more-dangerous/#.U6B7F41dWrw

SCIENCE OF HOW GMOs WORK ●────────────

Here is a good non-technical explanation:

"A gene consists at an average of about 3000 "code syllables". So it is a fairly large piece of information that is to be transferred.

1. The desired gene is taken out of the DNA of the donor cell. Special techniques are used, that are of no importance here.

2. A gene is much too small to be inserted with some kind of microsurgery. Therefore some carrier ("vector") is required which takes the gene into the recipient cell and somehow gets it inserted into the DNA of the recipient."

Keep reading here:

http://www.psrast.org/whisge.htm

And here is a crazy technical description:

http://www.nature.com/scitable/topicpage/genetically-modified-organisms-gmos-transgenic-crops-and-732
http://www.mrothery.co.uk/genetech/genetechnotes.htm

BT CORN

BT corn was one of the first big crops. The idea was to develop a gene that was resistant to caterpillars. You can read about it in depth here:

http://www2.ca.uky.edu/entomology/entfacts/ef130.asp

FLAVR SAVR TOMATOES

An interesting tale of an early flop in GMOs was this tomato. It's an amazing story about people trying to enter a business they know nothing about. Billions of dollars flushed down the drain. They wanted to make a bigger, juicer tomato that would have a longer shelf life, but it was too costly and didn't work as advertised.

http://www.public.iastate.edu/~rhetoric/105H16/cofp/tmrcofp.html

HOW COMPANIES ARE NOW GETTING AROUND REGULATION

Companies have adopted a new strategy in the GMO game. They are taking mass amounts of bio-mulch of a certain type of plant and searching for DNA that has specific traits in it. They're then isolating and using that DNA to clone and replicate it in plants. This means it's NOT GMO, because they're using a naturally occurring gene. Interesting here would be an aberrant gene discovered and used for whatever reasons. Ooooo, my nefarious mind wonders!

NATURAL DISASTERS

This is about a GMO released into the environment causing a disaster, but the information about naturally occurring ones and how the government reacts to them is relevant. I spent a lot of time researching how the government says they react to them and how they actually do. It's interesting stuff.

The reality is that governments don't react all that well or quickly to natural disasters. Part of this is unavoidable, as we often don't know when natural disasters will strike or how bad they'll be…but look at the pathetic response to Katrina and one has to wonder what they were doing.

http://www.sciencekids.co.nz/pictures/disasters.html

READY.GOV

This is actually a very useful site and lists out natural disasters, what you should do during them, etc. It's worth spending about an hour or so to read through it. Living in California we have earthquake kits and planned meeting places, etc. Every area seems to have its own prevalent natural disaster. Being prepared and having some sort of personal evacuation plan is key. Keep in mind; it may be days or weeks until someone else can help you, so learn to help yourself.

http://www.ready.gov/natural-disasters

FEMA

The Federal Emergency Management Agency has a mission statement that reads:

"FEMA's mission is to support our citizens and first responders to ensure that as a nation we work together to build, sustain, and improve our capability to prepare for, protect against, respond to, recover from, and mitigate all hazards."

They have broad-sweeping powers and can overrule civil liberties to achieve their goals, especially once a federal emergency zone has been declared. There are lots of conspiracy theories about FEMA. Some of them are fun, but most are BS.

2014 Budget: $9,590,000,000

http://www.fema.gov/

CONSPIRACIES

Concentration camps for the homeless and less desirables (which if you just drive around LA, you realize this isn't happening).

http://www.prisonplanet.com/fema-camps-city-to-exile-the-homeless-its-not-a-conspiracy-theory-anymore.html
http://conspiracy-watch.org/breaking-news-fema-camps-2014/

FDA

The U.S. Food and Drug Agency mission is:

"… responsible for protecting the public health by ensuring the safety, effectiveness, and security of human and veterinary drugs, biological products and medical devices; ensuring the safety of foods, cosmetics, and radiation-emitting products; and regulating tobacco products.

FDA is also responsible for advancing the public health by helping to speed innovations that make medicines more effective, safer, and more affordable and by helping the public get the accurate, science-based information they need to use medicines and foods to maintain and improve their health. FDA also has responsibility for regulating the manufacturing, marketing and distribution of tobacco products to protect the public health and to reduce tobacco use by minors."

2014 budget $4,653,657,000

http://www.fda.gov/downloads/AboutFDA/ReportsManualsForms/Reports/BudgetReports/UCM349710.pdf

CDC

Centers for Disease Control and Prevention are, of the three listed, my personal favorite. I know people that work for them, and despite the recent news about some viruses being not contained properly, they seem to really have their shit together.

The CDC mission statement:

"CDC works 24/7 to protect America from health, safety and security threats, both foreign and in the U.S. Whether diseases start at home or abroad, are chronic or acute, curable or preventable, human error or deliberate attack, CDC fights disease and supports communities and citizens to do the same.

CDC increases the health security of our nation. As the nation's health protection agency, CDC saves lives and protects people from health threats. To accomplish our mission, CDC conducts critical science and provides health information that protects our nation against expensive and dangerous health threats, and responds when these arise."

2014 Budget: $6,600,000,000

http://www.cdc.gov/

INTER AGENCY TASK FORCES

I had some difficulty finding out who would be in charge for a GMO-related disaster, I actually emailed a few contacts and was given different answers. FDA, CDC or FEMA... hmmm pick one. The best answer I could come up with was FEMA although the FDA claims to have jurisdiction over anything GMO-related. I could very well be wrong in how I depicted how this would work, but it was the best I had to work with based on the information that was available. Most of my scientist friends all seemed to agree that FEMA would take point so I went with the brain trust. It is interesting how certain things overlap. I've always been amazed too at how our government can be so good at certain things and so inept at others.

FIRE AS CATALYST FOR MUTATION

In the story I needed a reason for the GMO disaster to escalate and the only real way to do that was to have larger plants involved. Took me awhile to figure this one out, but in researching the fire itself and its effect it seemed to work. Wildfires are very important for plant growth and we've actually made them more intense by not allowing them to occur as regularly. It builds up and when it finally happens (as its natural cycle) they are more severe as a result of said buildup.

Some fires are beneficial, some are damaging - it all depends on the intensity.

"A healthy wildfire typically moves through the understory of a forest and burns the dead or dying plant material. This helps plant growth by destroying useless plant material and leaving healthy plant material intact. Pathogens on or around the plant are destroyed by the heat. Buildup of dead twigs and leaves is destroyed allowing new space for plants to grow. Following the fire, the increase in sunlight provided by removing the plant excess plant material helps the plants recover. Ash is absorbed into the soil, providing nutrients vital to plant growth. During a typical fire season (from July to October in California) when nitrogen is limited in the soil, the addition of organic plant matter to the soil can provide a source of nitrogen to boost plant growth."

http://www.ercsjsu.org/blog/category/native%20plant%20species

SINK HOLES

These and how they occur fascinate me. Scary as hell too! Can you imagine just sitting in your car or even in your house and one of these sucks you under and then fills in over you? You die and you may not even know how it happened. They happen mainly because of shifting earth and water movement underground, and sometimes because of collapsing underground caverns. All of these would be influenced by massive root systems growing under a city, so lots of those in LA during the fun.

http://science.howstuffworks.com/nature/natural-disasters/sinkhole.htm

SCHOLARLY ARTICLES ON GMO RISKS

I found this site biointegrity.org and lost about six hours skimming through and reading all of these. Some insane stuff here but fascinating to read. What I glean from it is basically no one knows what the long term effects of GMO are. There's also a nice differentiation in there from normal plant hybridization and the GMO processes.

http://www.biointegrity.org/FDAdocs/01/01.pdf
http://www.biointegrity.org/FDAdocs/03/03.pdf
http://www.biointegrity.org/FDAdocs/10/10.pdf

Thanks for picking up the finale of *Wildfire* Volume 1! Linda and I greatly appreciate you reading our work; it's been a pleasure doing this one. We are working on a sequel for next year.

"Hard to believe a dandelion caused all this."

I love this line and tossed it in there. Is the story that was laid out in *Wildfire* possible? I think so, yes, but maybe not to this dramatic extent. Could something get seeded into the biosphere that changes things for the worse permanently? You better believe it. I love the movie *Contagion*. If you've watched it, (SPOILER ALERT) you'll recall that the virus was caused by a bat pooping into a pig's lot. The pig was slaughtered and fed to Gwyneth Paltrow's character.

INVASIVE SPECIES ●

I talk about this on the last page as a "cautionary" tale. This has happened MANY times. Essentially someone brings, either knowingly or by accident, a bug, fish, or animal of some kind into a new environment where it didn't live before. This has massive effects on the local food chain, and can devastate entire species. This isn't speculation, it has happened many, many times. The first link has a long list of instances where this has happened.

http://www.invasivespeciesinfo.gov/animals/main.shtml

http://eol.org/info/460

JOURNALISM

I loathe modern news, so forgive me for putting that perspective in there. I gave it to Michelle Crawford, someone actually in the field. I think Michelle is actually my favorite character of the series. "Modern media defies ethics and justifies lies. And why? Because people don't want the real truth, they want sensationalism." The gossip and celebrity bait that people seem to want has zero interest to me. Most news organizations have also gutted their investigative reporting divisions today. There are very few true, free investigative reporters out there anymore. Why does this matter? Without Woodward and Bernstein (mentioned in the script) Watergate would NEVER have mattered, and Richard Nixon would not have resigned as President. If you've never seen *All the President's Men* with Robert Redford and Dustin Hoffman, you're missing out – it's a great flick.

Quote from Mark Zuckerburg (Facebook's founder), "A squirrel dying in front of your house may be more relevant to your interests right now than people dying in Africa."

This is a fascinating read, check this one out:

http://www.huffingtonpost.com/2014/05/22/facebook-media-rant_n_5374264.html

NO NARRATIVE

You've probably noticed that there is ZERO narrative in this book, and it was hard for me to do this way. One of the things I love about comic books is the internal narrative you can add to push the story along, info dump, or give an insight into what the character is thinking (I hate thought balloons). One reason I did this is that I really like this story, and am planning to spec it as a screenplay (my first official) for a film. No narrative in movies for the most part.

SHEILA'S DEATH

There are a lot of smart people that react poorly in extreme circumstances. I knew I was building this character to be unlikable and kill her off, but I've always been annoyed in movies when characters do stupid things. It's a trope of every horror film. There are studies showing that this is actually realistic for some people though, and since this woman was intended as cannon fodder, so be it!

TICKING CLOCK ENDING

I actually changed the ending. Originally I was planning on having an ending like *The Rock*, where they were flying in to bomb the city, but at the last minute Dan and his people are able to seed the newly mutated ACR to speed it up even further, so there's this tense few moments where we don't know how it'll end. This may have made a better dramatic ending, but it simply did not make sense logically with how the science would work. So forgive me…I went the way I did. There's already some implausible shit going on, I didn't want to push it too far.

SPEED UP THE PROCESS

Would this work? I took that kernel of an idea from a meeting I had with a Botany professor at UCR (Riverside, CA) who was complaining about fast growing species killing off entire areas of fauna. I wrote that down, along with a ton of other things from several meetings. I also sent the original outline to a couple specialists in this field, and they told me it was definitely unlikely, but possible. Hey, creative license! I'll take slimly possible. =)

Lastly, I want to say that this research and this story has CHANGED my opinion on GMOs. I was initially very pro-GMO, thinking people are being silly and crazy left-wing about it. I am not now anti-GMO, but I'm certainly slightly left of center. I'm for science and this research, but man…we need to test this stuff…and for decades. There are LONG term effects of things that we don't fully understand or grasp until they get out there. My lady smokes those e-cig things, and I see the people talking about how they "don't know" the effects of those over the long term. Things like that scare me, especially when it hits close to home.

Are GMOs partially culpable for heightened allergies, increases in cancer, and autoimmune afflictions? Are they contributing to the obesity epidemic? I really don't know, but I'll be safe over sorry, and maybe you should too. You can't avoid GMOs. It's just not realistic in the U.S. unless you're rich or live on an organic farm. But you can limit how much you eat of the overly processed, crazy sugar-enriched items that no one needs. Here are some more links for those of you that want to read up on the debate.

http://www.geneticliteracyproject.org/2014/07/01/anti-gmo-sentiments-lean-to-obsessive-in-arizona/

http://www.forbes.com/sites/jonentine/2013/10/14/2000-reasons-why-gmos-are-safe-to-eat-and-environmentally-sustainable/

http://thebirdman.org/Index/Others/Others-Doc-Environment&Ecology/+Doc-Environment&Ecology-FoodMatters/StimulatingPlantGrowthWithElectricity&Magnetism&Sound.htm

http://www.greenfacts.org/en/gmo/3-genetically-engineered-food/5-gene-flow.htm

http://www.ted.com/conversations/2694/genetic_manipulation_by_humani.html

That's it! Thanks for reading *Wildfire*! I hope you enjoyed it. We ARE doing a sequel and Linda will be returning to do the art with me. Very exciting stuff, look for it Fall 2015.

Carpe Diem!

Matt Hawkins
@topcowmatt
https://www.facebook.com/Selfloathingnarcissist

Cover Gallery

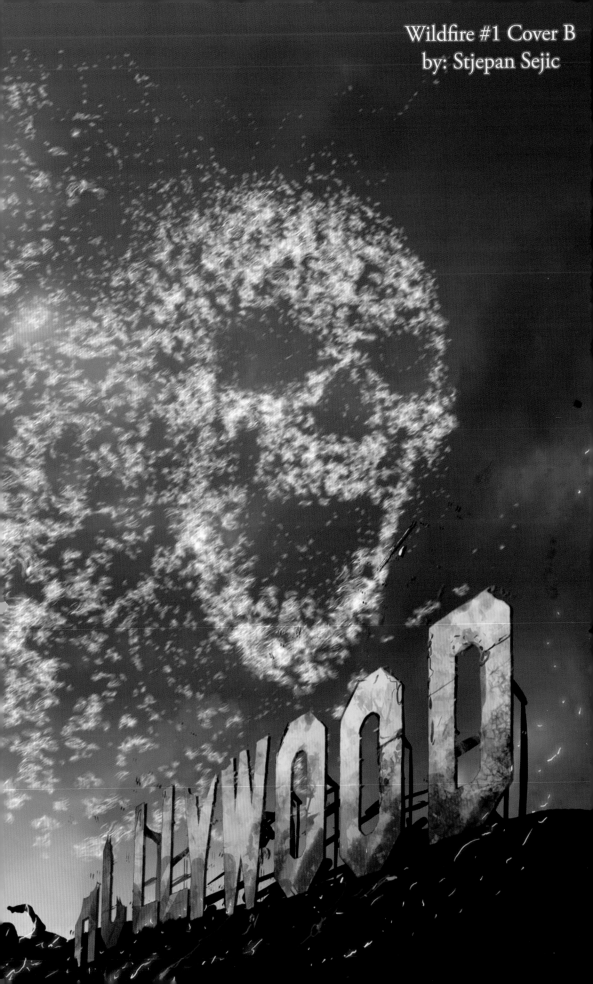

Wildfire #1 Cover B
by: Stjepan Sejic

Wildfire #1 Retailer Incentive
by: Linda Sejic

Wildfire #1 Phoenix Comic Con Variant
by: Linda Sejic

Wildfire #2 Cover A
by: Linda Sejic

Wildfire #2 Cover B
by: Stjepan Sejic

Wildfire #3 Cover A
by: Linda Sejic

Wildfire #3 Cover B
by: Stjepan Sejic

Wildfire #4 Cover B
by: Stjepan Sejic